D0174957

BEYOND
Selling

How To Maximize
Your Personal Influence

Dan S. Bagley III
AND
Edward J. Reese

Meta Publications
P. O. Box 565
Cupertino, California 95015

Library of Congress Card Number 87-063208
I.S.B.N. 0-916990-19-2

Typography by TLC Graphics

i

TABLE OF CONTENTS

Dedication

To Ann and Maryann

Acknowledgements

There are many people who have directly and indirectly aided in making this book come to life. First, much of it is based on the Neuro-Linguistic Programming work originally done by Richard Bandler and John Grinder. Its practical business applications are grounded in our direct contact with many excellent professionals, too numerous to mention here. Some, however, have given so freely in sharing their insights, philosophies and comments on the manuscript we wish to acknowledge them individually. Such associates, friends and colleagues as Andre DeZanger, Greg Stemm, John Morris, Robert Coates, Gregg Baron, Peter Berry, Marilyn Spechler, Jay Spechler and Richard Morales, M.D. have contributed greatly with encouragement, suggestions and deeds.

Finally, we'd like to acknowledge the tremendous patience, encouragement and support we received from our wives Ann and Maryann and our kids Drew and Jana, and Luanne and Valerie.

INTRODUCTION

If sales presentations were suits, some would instantly fit the prospect with comfort and elegance. And some would fit as if they were off the rack in someone else's size. Even if both styles had the same material, which one would you be inclined to buy?

A major difference between most salespeople and those few who are far superior is the influence strategies they use. Most have a relatively small, inflexible range of such strategies, and thus go through their sales day in hit-or-miss fashion, playing their numbers games based on fairly high sales ratios.

Yet others seem to sense quickly, if not immediately, how to size up a prospect and tailor their presentations to that particular prospect's individual buying strategy.

Historically this instant tailoring of rapport and influence has been considered an unexplainable gift, reserved for only a few fortunate souls. Early attempts at capturing this elusive quality were based on finding and identifying what traits constituted a "sales personality." Such attempts have been marginally successful. Other early attempts have been based on canned closing techniques aimed at breaking down the buyer's resistance. Though again marginally successful, these techniques often created more resistance than they overcame. They were seldom good for building long-term, repeat-business relationships.

Consultive selling and strategies for responding to buyer types have created movement in the right direction, but for many it has not been far enough in the right direction.

Recently, however, new technologies of personal and interpersonal influence have emerged based on behavioral psychology, linguistics, and communication models. The result of these new technologies is a learnable system for gently and rapidly establishing meaningful levels of rapport and sales influence.

These technologies create communication synergy between the salesperson and the prospect in such a way as to establish nearly instant rapport and logical understanding. These technologies go beyond the hit-or-miss approaches of the past, and go directly to what has always made the great salespeople great.

The skills that work today have always worked. What's new are the technologies for recognizing and teaching them in a way that assures a positive difference.

The new influence technologies enhance, improve, and expand upon the successful aspects of what has historically been sales training. And in doing so they help already successful salespeople to become more successful through understanding, appreciating, and further developing the key elements that they did naturally and unconsciously.

For those who have not yet found their peak ranges, these technologies provide step-by-step methods:

1. for establishing immediate rapport;
2. for ascertaining what the prospect really wants;
3. for turning objections around to selling points without seeming confrontive or pushy;
4. for making trial closes through body language alone;
5. for being able to unlock the prospect's personal buying strategies through simple questioning techniques;
6. for using covert suggestions and commands for coming to an agreement, and much more.

Of course, such strides forward require a framework through which to learn, understand and remember. Too often sales models are so complicated that they are not useful where they count most—in the field.

The model and approaches you learn here are scientifically based, professionally proven, intuitively understandable, and easily remembered. Additionally, while many books and programs speak in generalities such as, "Immediately try to establish rapport with your prospect..." here you will receive a step-by-step means for effectively establishing rapport on many levels.

The broad model to help you achieve new levels of successful selling has ten elements. They are:

1. Gain Rapport
2. Identify Needs
3. Establish Criteria
4. Harness Objectives
5. Check Rapport
6. Offer Plan
7. Gather Objections
8. Respond Appropriately
9. Request Action
10. Follow up Every Lead

While the ten steps are a simple framework on which to build, remembering these ten components is even simpler once we chunk them into five logical, easy-to-recall-and-review pieces.

They are:

1. GRIN (Gain Rapport, Identify Needs)
2. ECHO (Establish Criteria, Harness Objectives)
3. CROP (Check Rapport, Offer Plan)
4. GO RA RA (Gather Objections, Respond Appropriately, Request Action)
5. FUEL (Follow Up Every Lead)

So what's the first thing to do when you greet a new prospect? That's right, GRIN. You've heard of reflective listening, haven't you? So the next thing to remember is ECHO. As you narrow down the possibilities by going from general to more and more specific (snipping away the parts that are unnecessary to your persuasive progress) you CROP. And then to culminate the sales experience you GO RA RA! After the sale is made it is important to keep the relationship burning so you FUEL. That, by the way, includes the hottest leads of the moment, which are those leads your customer has given about his or her own present and future needs.

Gain Rapport, Identify Needs, Establish Criteria, Harness Objectives, Check Rapport, Offer Plan, Gather Objections, Respond Appropriately, Request Action, and Follow Up Every Lead are the component parts of a simple model. But in its simplicity there are profound insights to recognize, learn and apply.

Much of what we present here you will immediately grasp, visualize and agree with. You'll see yourself in similar situations and hear yourself saying, "Yeah, that's right. It matches what I know to be true."

Some other parts you read and mentally experience here will initially make you pause and question how they fit into your frame of reference. You won't immediately have a handle on them, and as you reflect you'll initially ask yourself if they truly relate to you and your individual selling situations. Then as a few moments pass you'll suddenly see how those points relate to you and you'll hear yourself agreeing yet again as the applications and benefits become clear to you.

If this book is to be a true learning and growth experience there will be yet other parts that you will initially question and doubt significantly, even to the point of mentally writing them off as you grapple with the concept and try to see yourself succeeding in such scenarios. Yet sometime later, perhaps when driving down an interstate highway where your mind wanders into territories of new thoughts and innovative ideas as the rhythm of the road lulls away the minutes, you'll suddenly experience a flash of insight. You will discover a new way to approach a sales problem you have been wrestling with for some time. And as you congratulate yourself on the excellent plan that has suddenly filled your mind, you may not even recall where the seed of this new bloom was possibly first planted.

To facilitate your understanding and application of the concepts presented here we offer diverse examples from many selling and non-selling situations. We additionally conclude each chapter with our answers to clarification questions we're occasionally asked in our seminars.

If you actively participate and project yourself into this book, actually applying what you learn, you will harvest an enormous amount of additional momentum and enjoyment in your business relationships, your personal relationships and the hundreds of small encounters where persuasion and personal power are important.

Good luck on this new adventure as you explore *Beyond Selling*.

CHAPTER ONE

The Changing Game

THE CHANGING GAME

Have you noticed that selling today is different than it has been in years past? So many of the old manipulative techniques of yesteryear, such as high pressure and quick closes, are no longer appropriate in today's business environment. Consumers and buyers are evolving and getting more sophisticated. They are making more demands and are no longer responding to the hackneyed, tried-and-true closing techniques that seemed to work so well years ago. And just as customers are evolving, our methods of interacting with those customers and clients need to evolve also. As people get more sophisticated, those of us in the business of influencing also need to become more skillful. We need to pay closer attention to our clients to make sure we understand what they need on many levels before trying to influence them to make purchase decisions.

The answer isn't simply in better selling. The answer lies *Beyond Selling*. To influence purchase decisions today we need to do more than simply supply products and services in neat little need satisfaction packages. We need to respond to more than simply how people buy. We need to respond to their varied communication and thinking patterns. In doing so, we can make and accelerate our own success.

It's time for the barriers that have been erected between buyers and sellers, influencers and those who are influenced, to come down. These are barriers that have been created by short-term manipulative techniques; the short-term benefits have principally been centered around the needs of the seller rather than the needs of the buyer.

In *Megatrends*, John Naisbitt devotes an entire chapter to long-term versus short term gains in the areas of management and company philosophy. Sales and marketing are no different. Most of today's business success is based on long term customer satisfaction, which leads to referrals and repeat business even when the purchase cycle is long.

For example, I recently was looking for a good reliable automobile. The search led me to a high priced luxury American made diesel. The salesperson assured me that the car would be extremely reliable, the engine would run for 150,000 miles and the repairs would be minimal.

After fourteen service department visits in the first year (including four towings) it became obvious that the car was not reliable.

With each service call, my anger at the salesperson and the dealership increased in geometric progressions to the point where I presently drive a high-performance foreign car.

When purchasing my new car, the salesperson spent a great deal of time interviewing me and found that I not only valued reliability but also luxury and performance. The salesperson was careful to point out that because of the high performance qualities of the car, each system had a backup system for the safety of my family members and myself.

The salesperson also added that because of these double safety systems and the high-performance factors, I could expect to visit the service center at least several times a year.

His statements were true. During the first year the car was in the shop for service more than a dozen times. But this time with each visit the service department reinforced the idea that they were keeping up both the safety and performance factors in the car.

Because of their approach, I felt cared for and continue to enjoy the car and appreciate the dealership.

Now, which of these dealerships do you think has gotten my referrals and will continue to get my business in the future?

A global example of the importance of long-term customer satisfaction is demonstrated in McDonald's success story. Ray Kroc built his McDonald's empire on a foundation of quality, service, cleanliness and value—all long term attributes. If an order of fries was overcooked he demanded that they be thrown out. If a bun got a thumb gouge, it was tossed out rather than served. He realized that a McDonald's hamburger served in Newark could reflect on his organization throughout the world. His marketing scope was infinitely broader than a hamburger and an order of fries sold to a customer today.

Perhaps you have experienced entering a restaurant alone for dinner and having the hostess ask in a flat, unenthusiastic tone, "Only one?"

If so, how did you feel at that moment? Welcomed? Anxious to come back with a bunch of your friends? Is this a place you'd enjoy bringing your customers to? Probably not.

In this case the hostess's short-term perception of your economic value undermined the foundation for repeat business.

These three examples demonstrate just one common barrier to effective selling—a short-term versus long-term perspective. But there are more—many more obstacles—to recognize and overcome.

The techniques, strategies, and insights shared in this book are extremely powerful in terms of their ability to add to your personal power and to your ability to exert influence over others. They are well grounded in social and psychological theory, and well proved where it counts most: in the business arena. Some sales professionals have intuitively developed these skills and techniques and through trial and error have become masters. Many more, however, have learned them through a broad spectrum of education, training and practice.

What we provide here is the education and training. What you provide is the practice. What we are offering here is truly beyond what most have conceived of as selling. Yet it's not so far beyond that it doesn't relate to many of the good things you have already been doing. What you learn here will not only dramatically increase your ability to influence others, but it will also add greatly to your enjoyment of your role as a salesperson.

If you are already in the top one or two percent of salespeople then you are going to recognize a lot of what we offer here. And you will come to a greater appreciation and understanding of just what it is that is making you do so well. If you are in the upper 20 percent of all salespeople, then what we present here will not only reinforce what you are already doing well, but it will also give you some additional insights that you have perhaps intuited but not yet conceptualized. When you apply these you will find your own performance surging as if a turbo charge had suddenly been put on your success vehicle. If you are in the top 50 percent of all salespeople then you have probably already built a pretty good foundation. While many things are still hit-and-miss, you are well on your way to making major leaps forward and achieving those great goals that have been sparkling and calling you from just out of reach. What you will learn will fit quite nicely with what you already know, yet you will be adding dimensions of influence and success that once seemed reserved for people other than you. If you are not yet in the top 50 percent of all salespeople then you have the biggest upside potential of all. Chances are you are already doing a number of things right, and there is a good possibility that you are doing a number of other things that are limiting your forward movement. Persevere, my friend, to paraphrase the philosopher William James, there's very little difference between one person and another, but what little there is can be very important.

We are concerned with the differences that make the difference. If you will learn, apply and practice the concepts presented here, you will go beyond any level of success you have already experienced. What we are presenting to you is a blueprint for maximizing your personal influence. It is a blueprint for moving you beyond selling as you have known it in the past.

SENSORY-SPECIFIC STATEMENTS

First, decide what you really want. Sure you want success, but that's too vague. In stating what you want you need to state it in sensory specific terms that you can see, hear, feel, taste, touch, smell, or count. In other words, your outcome needs to be measurable.

Have you ever played out this conversation with a friend?

"What are you hungry for?"

"Anything's okay with me."

"Good. What about Chinese food?"

"Naw, I'm not really in the mood for Chinese."

"What about Mexican, then?"

"Let's not do that this time."

"Okay, what would you like?"

"Anything, just so it's good."

Note how the lack of specific sensory-based information interferes with achieving a satisfactory outcome. Unfortunately, business decisions and life decisions work just like lunch decisions. To get what you want you must get specific.

ACCENT ON THE POSITIVE

The next step for truly establishing what you want is to state your outcomes in positive terms. For example, "I don't want to smoke any more," is not a well stated objective. The reason is simple. It's virtually impossible for the mind to concentrate effectively on the reverse of an idea. To think of not smoking, you first have to think of smoking. To think of not eating, you first have to think of eating. If you have ever tried to lose weight by saying to yourself, "I will not eat, I am not going to eat, I am not hungry, I will not eat," you have probably found your own words drove you to incredible levels of hunger. Many people who have tried this strategy have found that they actually gained weight because they became so obsessed with not eating that food was always on their minds.

Our minds are much more powerful than our discipline can ever be. The key is controlling our minds. In this book you will learn specific ways of maintaining your focus in doing just that. Skeptical? Try this. You've probably made it through the entire day to this point without thinking of an elephant, so I'll ask you just to go for another three minutes keeping that elephant completely out of your mind. Use as much discipline as you can, but don't flash an image of an elephant in your mind. While you are keeping that image of the elephant out of your mind, for goodness sake, don't put a monkey on his back riding and waving at you. And while you are not having that little monkey riding on the elephant's back, be sure you don't put a yellow hat on the little monkey's head that you are not thinking about.

As you can readily see, by suggesting what I don't want you to do I am bringing that very thing about. The bottom line is you need to concentrate on what you do want, not on what you don't want. In the case of non-smoking, the key is to concentrate on clean healthy lungs, breathing clearly, feeling high energy, seeing your loved ones smile at you with pride at your healthy lifestyle, etc.

Have you ever said to a client, "I don't want you to worry about delivery," and had the delivery concern become an obstacle? Have you ever concentrated on not sounding nervous to the point that your voice began to crack? Have you ever tried not focusing on your customer's distracting idiosyncrasies only to have them monopolize your attention? Then you understand the point.

THE EVIDENCE PROCEDURE

Once you have your outcome stated in positive terms you'll need an evidence procedure. In other words, how will you know when you've achieved your personal goal? What will you see? What will you hear? What will you feel? If your sensory- specific goal is, I want economic strength and I will know I have it when I have $200,000 in income, you need to bring it to life on as many levels as you can. Will you see the checks? What else will you see? Will you see how people look at you differently? Will you see yourself driving a different type of car? What will you hear? What will you say to yourself? What will others say to you? What will others say about you? What will you feel inside?

Fantasize that for a moment. Imagine yourself walking down the street, feeling the way you will feel when you reach your success goal. What are you wearing? Is there anyone walking with you? Where are you going? Again, bring it to life on as many levels as you can.

THE CONGRUENCY PRINCIPLE

In deciding what you truly want, make sure you are congruent. Make sure it matches what you *really* want, not simply what you *should* want. If there is some little voice inside you saying to this "Nah, that wouldn't be me," you need to investigate a little bit further. What are your personal priorities? Maybe it's more time with the family, maybe it's a little more leisure time. You need to decide up front what you really, truly want. Otherwise you're going to play endless games with yourself, running a little ways in one direction, and a little ways in the other.

Let's go back to the goal of $200,000 a year in sales. It stands to reason that such a surge forward will require some psychological risk-taking, such as many more high level presentations. Here's where procrastination might set in because such a commitment may well take away from leisure time, family activities and safe time in your comfort zone of familiar activities.

Unless dealt with up front, these incongruities will become arenas of endless game playing where your energy and thoughts become dissipated through conflicting directions.

Many sales managers have mentioned this problem of incongruity (demonstrated by procrastination and low commissions). In fact, it has been cited repeatedly as a prime cause of a salesperson's inability to move up the ladder.

Perhaps you've heard such comments as: "His head seems to be somewhere else," or "He seems to be more worried about his next vacation than completing this project," or "She spends more time worrying about problems than solving them."

THE INTEGRITY FACTOR

Integrity is incredibly important when achieving the levels of influence that can take you wherever you want to go. Integrity means more than just staying inside the limit of the law. It means more than staying within the limits of honesty. Integrity is more than not lying to other people. Integrity involves caring enough about other people to learn and understand *their* outcomes, goals, and objectives before influencing them into helping achieve *our* goals, outcomes and objectives.

The integrity factor is the creative part that can create win-win scenarios rather than win-lose scenarios within selling and influence arenas. We have seen this so clearly again and again as we study high achievers across this country. They typically sell from a "you perspective." Their mind set is based on what the other person wants. Then they match their clients' outcomes with what they want. Finally, they simply meld the two objectives into one win-win plan.

Mary Kay Ashe exemplifies this point. In 1983, Mary Kay Cosmetics celebrated its 20th anniversary with annual sales over $300 million. In speaking of her more than 200,000 beauty consultants (some earning more than $50,000 a year) in her book *Mary Kay on People Management* (Warner Books, 1984) she states, "These remarkable sales professionals have succeeded not through the 'dog eat dog' competition so commonplace in 'big business,' but through a sensitivity for the needs of others... We have intentionally developed a unique managerial concept that allows fairness to flourish in business."

From Mary Kay Ashe to Mo Siegel, founder and moving force behind Celestial Seasonings, to Lee Iacocca of Chrysler, we find tough-but-fair influence strategies that allow the benefits of winning to be shared in business transactions.

Of course, not everyone who has achieved economic and social success through influencing others has been a good guy. But over time, society has a way of catching up with the shortcutters, of undermining the chiselers and of sapping the strength and energy of those who have built their empires in such a way that they no longer can trust anyone around them. Alfred Korzybski, the father of general semantics, observed, "God may forgive our sins but our nervous systems won't." Al Capp, speaking through his cartoon character Mammy Yokum, was fond of observing, "Good is better than evil cause it's so much nicer." In the area of powerful influence techniques, it's also good business.

THE REALITY FACTOR

Behavior is simply a function of the values, beliefs, needs and habits any person has. If you understand a person's values, beliefs, needs and habits you will start seeing patterns. When you understand the patterns you are in the inner workings of their values, beliefs, needs and habits. Actually, these values, beliefs, needs and habits don't really *show us* reality so much as *create* reality. Consider this: it's during the winter months and you've caught something that feels remarkably like the flu. Your head's all stopped up, and you feel achy. When you go to your medicine cabinet you find you have no appropriate medicine. With a runny nose you get into your car, and you start driving through the drizzly sleet to the nearest shopping area. You can hardly believe your good luck. There, right in front of the drugstore, are two spaces. As you start moving towards those two spaces, a car comes whizzing past you and wheels in diagonally, blocking both of those spaces. The driver jumps out and runs into the drugstore.

How do you feel at this point about that person? What would you like to do to that person? What would you like to say to that person? What type of person would do something like that to you?

Let's continue: You finally find another space that happens to be about 22 spaces from the front; it's so miserable outside that you shudder at having to run up to the drugstore from even that far out. But you do it anyway. By the time you get up to where the car had pulled in, you notice that in the time it took you to get to your space the person has already gone in, done business, and left. Now how do you feel toward that person? It's probably amplified, isn't it? And now you perhaps not only know what type of person that is but know some things about his or her parentage.

As you go into the drugstore you notice that the check-out clerk seems shaken and pale. You turn to the clerk, ask what is the problem, and the clerk replies, "Oh, a man came running in here just a moment ago and used the phone to call 911, the ambulance service. It seems there has been a terrible accident down the road and he was calling for help. He's raced back there to see if he can give additional first aid.He's afraid someone may die before the ambulance gets there."

Now how do you feel toward that person? What's changed? Simply more information. Additional insight. We create our realities with insufficient information. When someone cuts us off in traffic, we often respond as if he got up that morning to make our day less happy. When a client is short with us, we sometimes react as if that client is a bad person, rather than a person having a bad day.

For example, a client of ours had completed a major presentation of customized promotional clocks that he felt was going to result in his largest order of the year. However, after a week the purchase order was not forthcoming. He called repeatedly, but got no return phone call. He wrote a nice letter but got no response. Three weeks passed and panic set in.

"I must have offended the client in some manner," he confided to us. "Do you think I should apologize and ask what I did? After all, we're talking about a sizable order here."

"How do you know he's simply not procrastinating?" we asked.

"I don't know for sure, but why wouldn't he even return a quick call if he weren't angry?" our client asked.

We prevailed on our client to get on a plane, go to the office with no appointment, under the pretense that he was in town for the day and needed only ten minutes to follow up on the order.

When the client saw him he immediately welcomed him and apologized profusely for the delay. He had indeed procrastinated and was now ready to place the order.

INFLUENCING YOUR OWN MOTIVATION

Before you can influence others you must be able to influence yourself. Remember, achieving success is an inside job. Motivation is inside your head.

It's been many years since we first saw a tee shirt with the saying, "I've abandoned my search for reality and would now settle for a good fantasy." Since seeing that we've come to realize that there is not only humor in that statement but also a profound message, for since we create our own reality based on our own values, our own beliefs, our own needs and our own habits, then in a sense our reality is based largely on what we imagine. We're often dealing in fantasies. Just for insight let's think in terms of functional fantasies versus dysfunctional fantasies. The reason we don't call them rules or laws is we're not sure that they're absolutely true. What we have noticed is there are certain beliefs that appear fairly consistently in high achievers.

At this point it becomes obvious that the gathering of sensory-specific information gives you the absolute advantage of learning more about your clients and their needs. Reality then becomes the ability to know more and mind read less.

Of course, even the best of influenced professionals occasionally gets stumped through mind reading without verifying. Advertising's great David Ogilvy enjoys telling the story of his early encounter with promoting Dove soap. His idea was to position the product as totally different from ordinary soaps. In doing so, his print ads ran the slogan, "Dove Makes Soap

Obsolete." His mind reading assumption was that people were educated enough to at least understand his slogan. However, readership studies showed that 40% of his market did not know what the word "obsolete" meant.

In the absence of sensory-specific information providing facts about our prospects, we're only able to guess at where our best influence thrusts reside.

We've already discussed five very important values that these high achievers tend to have: 1) long term versus short-term perspectives 2) positively stated outcomes 3) clear evidence procedures 4) integrity 5) information gathering skills.

Now let's investigate some specific beliefs, which we'll call "functional fantasies." While not all performers have all of these beliefs, most have many of them.

FUNCTIONAL FANTASIES

First, *anything worth doing, is worth doing*, what? Chances are you said something like *"well."* And that's what most people believe, including high achievers. Yet the other side of that coin is the point that is truly worth knowing. That is, *anything worth doing, is worth doing badly.* Was it worth learning how to walk? I certainly hope so. When you learned to walk, did you learn to walk all in one try, or did you fall once? Or did you fall down twice? Or did you fall down dozens and dozens and dozens of times before you first tottered across a room successfully? Clearly, anything worth doing is worth doing badly until we learn how to do it well.

Consider Johnson and Johnson's Tylenol dilemma. When the poisoning started they found themselves in big trouble. Product tampering had never been a major problem before, but they accepted responsibility and moved forward to correct the tampering problems responsibly.

A lesser company might have folded and given the brand name up as a loser. But today Johnson and Johnson's Tylenol is considered a winner, not a loser. And what they learned and utilized from that adversity is what gave them that edge.

Recently one of our friends got into the interior landscaping business. She had gone on seven unsuccessful cold calls. We had the opportunity of speaking with one of the clients she had been unsuccessful with.

He reported that she had a strong bias toward live versus artificial plants and had made a number of unconscious facial grimaces as he proudly showed her his artificial plants.

After we shared with her the comments about her grimacing, she at first reacted with surprise and disbelief and said, "Oh, I wouldn't do that." After a few moments of further discussion she admitted, "Well, maybe I did that and wasn't aware of it." After a few more minutes she decided to return and smile at his artificial plants.

Since that time she has learned to appear to appreciate artificial plants as part of interior plantscaping. In six months her sales have increased eightfold.

In each of these cases setbacks have provided valuable learning insights that strengthened the system or the individual.

Think about one of your own past *failures*. Was there ever a time you blew a sale through not closing effectively? Was there ever a time you didn't handle a client's anger well? Was there ever a time that you misjudged a prospect's predispositions to the point of missing an economic opportunity?

The school of hard knocks has tough but effective teachers. So what did you learn from these setbacks? Do you now know how to close more effectively? Have you reconsidered how to better handle a customer's anger? Do you now watch more intently for cues that signal your prospect's predispositions?

If the answers to these questions are yes, then your success mechanisms are operating more effectively now. The setback gave you the feedback to do better in the future. Plus, since you're constantly calling on more people, you're able to use your

new insights in a multiplier effect. In other words, the insights
you gained in one defeat are in place to help you achieve
victories in many more situations. There is no failure. There's
only feedback.

Think about it: If you pay attention and learn from your
mistakes, falling short of a worthwhile goal doesn't make you a
failure any more than eating carrots makes you a rabbit.

The second functional fantasy is *I am responsible for my
own outcomes.* For example, I am responsible for my own
happiness, I am responsible for my own success, I am responsible for my own peace of mind. Is this true? Well, let's call it a
functional fantasy. But, if you believe it, you will never again
believe yourself to be a drowning victim in a sea of
circumstance.

Recently I was in San Francisco visiting some friends. On a
particular morning, I was riding in the front seat on the
passenger side, when my friend realized she needed to get some
gasoline from one of the very small gas stations in that area. As
she pulled in, I couldn't help but notice a most unfortunate,
unpleasant looking woman seemingly scowling at the whole
world as she pumped her gas. My friend eased around her car,
backed up, and got out to start pumping her gas. Meanwhile,
the unpleasant lady had finished her pumping, paid and had
gotten in the car and started to move around us. She then got
out and called, "Hey, you have to move your car over to the left.
You're blocking my way." There was, frankly, plenty of room
for her to get around, but my friend smiled and said, "I'm sorry I
blocked your way," moved the car a little bit closer to the curb,
and resumed pumping the gas. As the woman edged past in
excruciatingly tense, slow maneuvers, there was so much distance between our cars that I couldn't help but notice that in
closing her door, she had left her coat hanging out and dragging the ground. As she passed by, I simply said, "Excuse me,
ma'am, but I notice your coat is dragging the ground. It looks
like it may do damage if you don't pull it in." She gave me a

scowl as if to say, "What business is it of yours?" Then she opened her door, yanked her coat inside, and resumed her slow, excruciating squeeze around our car. It was at that moment I noticed that she had left her gas cap on the back of her trunk.

Now I was faced with a dilemma. Here was a woman who had twice offended me; once by her existence on Earth, shown by her horrible expressions at everybody around her, and the second time when I tried to be nice to her but she had snubbed me. At this next point, in order to help her I had to jump from the car and go chase after her. I was faced with a decision.

What would you have done at this point? I wish I could say it was total altruism that made me leap from the car and chase her down, but, quite frankly, it was a combination of curiosity at how she would react, and a sudden flash of realization that I could not let her be in charge of my behavior. I could not let her unpleasant behavior dictate my style of living. I indeed leaped out and caught her before she entered traffic, calling, "Lady, you left your gas cap on the back. Let me put it in for you." As I fumbled to get her gas cap on, she got out of her car, came back, took it from my hand, and said, "Here, I know how to do it," and put on her own gas cap. She turned, started to get in the car, and looked back with a truly gentle smile. She said, "Thank you. I appreciate your help." I smiled and felt great about it. But the important part wasn't the thanks. The important part was the realization about who was in charge of my good day. We simply cannot afford to let every crazy person, every unpleasant encounter, every rude prospect we encounter make or break our days. We have to be responsible for our own outcomes.

One of my clients is GE Plastics. Within their sales organization is a young woman named Nancy. As a trainee, it was her job to solicit and develop new, smaller accounts through cold calls. One molder she called on was immediately hostile. A decade earlier, when he was first getting started, GE had not considered him a good enough credit risk to sell to him on an open account. His attitude was, "So now that I'm successful you finally want my business, huh?"

It took her months of calling on him to finally melt down the ten years of resentment he had carried. She finally received a $20,000 order from him. It was a small but good start.

Then lightning struck. When accounting checked and found no current records on the molder, they called him to say that they would not extend credit to him until after he had gotten established with them.

In a fit of rage he told accounting what they could do with his order, adding that he would never ever do business with the company again.

Now answer this. Who was responsible for this client's decision—Nancy or accounting? There's more. When Nancy heard the terrible news that afternoon, she immediately called the angry molder.

"I called for two reasons," she said. "First, I want to apologize for the mistake. And, second, I want you to know that I still expect to earn your business."

Granted, at that moment, she took some tough knocks on the phone. But several months later she had re-established rapport and was finally getting orders from this molder. What was the turning point? "She earned my respect that day I was so angry," the molder later confided to Nancy's boss. "As mad as I was, I didn't expect any sales rep would have the courage to face me."

Who was responsible for the client's decision, Nancy or accounting?

In this case, Nancy took responsibility for herself by going back to the customer and selling him on her determination to be of service. Just think how easy it would have been for her to get angry, depressed, or discouraged and blame accounting for her loss of the sale.

Thus you can see how this second functional fantasy of taking responsibility for your own outcomes can be applied even when the you-know-what hits the fan.

This raises the question of what happens when we're not feeling up to giving a challenging opportunity our best shot? All humans have bad days, don't they?

Sure they do. But, that still does not change who is responsible for your outcomes. How many times have you witnessed an athlete turn in one of his or her best performances in spite of injury? From small Nadia Comaneci to any number of NFL players, we've seen scores of athletes of all shapes and sizes rise to great accomplishments in spite of physical and mental ootbacks.

Are there techniques of how to do this consistently? You bet there are. And you'll be learning these as we continue. As consultants we have each given international seminars while overriding a burning fever without having anyone in our audiences suspect we were anything less than 100 percent.

If you're on the road a lot, you no doubt encounter an incredible number of situations that could potentially derail your momentum—late planes, uncomfortable pillows, jet lag, differing styles of doing business, misfiring alarm clocks, upsetting food, cultural differences, and timing miscalculation, to name a few. Yet with each of these adversities you're faced with a choice: to take responsibility for your behavior and achieve your outcome, or not to take responsibility and allow yourself the luxury of failing and blaming the results on circumstance or the ubiquitous "them."

The third functional fantasy is *Work is Play*. Recently I was in Las Vegas at the Bally Hotel conducting three seminar sessions for several thousand AFS florists. The morning of my presentations I found myself once again up at 4:00 a.m. (an hour ahead of my wake-up call) tingling with excited anticipation of the fun, challenging day ahead as I imagined the groups and their positive reactions to what we would do together. As I put some finishing touches on my presentation, the anticipation grew. Breakfast at 6:00 a.m. was delicious as each bite seemed to fuel my day's momentum. By 7:00 a.m. when I made the final check on the staging, the familiar feeling of adrenalin pumping through my system was fully evident to me. By 8:00 a.m. everything had been checked, adjusted and rechecked, and the challenge now was to hold my own excitement in balance with my presentation and audience.

During the last hour before the seminar started, one of the setup people sidled up to me and said, "I guess you'll be pretty glad when this is all over and you can get out and have some fun."

"What a surprising thing to say!" I thought. Here in the midst of excitement, suspense, the chance to succeed or fail, the chance to help my client achieve predetermined worthwhile objectives, the chance to affect people's lives positively, all in a high-stakes game involving ego, reputation and future economic and psychological payoffs, someone was talking to me about getting out to have some fun!

His comment immediately triggered my memory back to a time that I hadn't thought of in years. I was sixteen and that summer I was doing my first selling in the business world, working for my father selling specialty advertising. It was terribly hot that summer, and since my selling skills were more terrible than hot, I was discouraged.

It was a Friday afternoon about 4:30 and I was back in the office, having just completed a fairly poor week. I ambled into my dad's office and plopped down in a chair across the room from him, stretching my legs out in my most discontented teenager pose. He was at his desk finishing the paperwork on the large amount of business he had written that day. He looked up and said, "You know, I just love this business. I love getting out and meeting people, seeing lots of established friends, and being able to help them. I love the excitement of not knowing what I'm going to make, but knowing I can make it a lot. I love the ability to call on whoever I want, whenever I want, setting my own pace and my own hours. And I love the chance to be creative in my advertising and selling ideas. This is a great business to be in."

"Sure," I shot back, feeling defensive. "I'd love it too if I were making as much as you are."

He laughed out loud, looked me in the eye and said, "Son, I loved it *before* the money was great. *The money is a byproduct of doing what you love exceptionally well.*"

It was years before I truly understood and lived his words. But here I was in Las Vegas about to present life-changing ideas to thousands of people and sell them on taking certain actions to improve their ability to sell their products, and I was once again experiencing the familiar excitement of doing something that I love.

After reflecting a moment I smiled broadly at the man who had suggested I might be looking forward to getting through the task at hand to get out and have some fun. "That'll be fun, all right," I acknowledged, "but *this* is the *real* fun!"

The CEO of Lord & Taylor, Joseph Brooks, once advised, "Find what makes you tingle." In other words, one key to success is to love what you do so much that it makes you tingle in anticipation. And a key to loving what you do is to do what you love—do what makes you tingle.

Do you enjoy conquests? Do you like big payoffs? Do you enjoy helping others? Do you enjoy being in control of your time? Do you enjoy competition? Do you enjoy the comradeship of working with other people? Do you enjoy building relationships? Do you enjoy working with ideas? Problem solving? Do you like the idea of personally benefiting in approximate proportion to benefiting others? Do you enjoy the thrill of winning? Do you like the feeling of self improvement? Do you ever fantasize how good you'd really be if you stayed a little more focused on what is important in your business life?

The fourth functional fantasy we commonly find in very high achievers is *in every adversity are hidden the seeds of victory*. This is more than every cloud has a silver lining. It also includes:

A. There's excitement in challenge.
B. Every obstacle has productive answers and insights if we'll creatively and energetically seek them.
C. Working through challenges strengthens us for greater challenges.
D. Many of the best lessons in life are learned in the University of Hard Knocks.
E. The game isn't over until it's over... and probably not even then.

Let's briefly consider these subcategories one at a time. There *is* excitement in challenge. That's why we go to sporting events to identify with and cheer for our team. Additionally, if activities are not challenging we quickly lose interest.

Think how often you get ready to take on a challenge and feel a surge of excitement charge through your body. Now if the task at hand were so easy anyone could handle it, where would that surge be? Admit it. You love the excitement, don't you? Smile to yourself if that's basically true for you.

But setbacks do occur. They're part of the game. And as you know from your past, when you have experienced and overcome adversity you have within you a new level of confidence in knowing that you are all the smarter.

Even disasters can be productive. In our seminars we occasionally encourage participants to discuss their productive disasters. Productive disasters are those major setbacks that turn out to be major positive turning points in one's life. Sometimes the productivity comes from realizing past mistakes. Sometimes it comes from being placed in an entrepreneurial role through necessity. Sometimes the productivity comes through the character-building nature of picking oneself up and redoubling the efforts.

Such adversity can hurt, but it lays the basis for ordinary people striving a little more effectively to do extraordinary things and, in doing so, becoming extraordinary people. Henry Ford, for example, went bankrupt twice before hitting it as an automobile magnate. Abraham Lincoln lost 23 out of 26 elections and at one time was suicidal. But his adversities, depression, and heartache shaped him into one of the greatest presidents our country has ever known. Tom Dempsey learned to be the greatest field goal kicker of his time while kicking with only half a foot. I recently had dinner with Lee Lanktree, the founder of the highly successful Twistee Treat ice cream franchise. That day he had made a million dollar franchise sale. I was quizzing him about his phenomenal success with this franchising endeavor and asked if he had been involved in many franchising endeavors before. He had been involved in more than thirty before finding his true range with this one.

The fifth functional fantasy is *things don't get better by accident; they get better by appropriate action.* How many times have you heard mediocre salespeople say, "Man, I can't wait until times get better" or "I hope these problems go away or I'm not going to make any money." High achievers take the necessary appropriate actions to make them go away. They understand that problems that go away by themselves tend to come back by themselves.

The story is told in sports circles about a writer who had visited Jack London Park and then went to see Kenny Stabler, then quarterback for the Oakland Raiders. The writer wanted to see if the fire that burned in Jack London's heart was to be found in such winners as Stabler. To investigate this he took a quotation from Jack London and read it to Stabler as he was getting dressed after a game. The quotation read, "I would rather be ashes than dust. I would rather my spark should burn out in a brilliant blaze than it should be stifled by dry rot. I would rather be a superb meteor every atom of me in a magnificent glow than a sleepy impermanent planet. The proper function of man is to live, not to exist. I shall not waste my days in trying to prolong them. I shall use my time." Upon reading this to Stabler he said, "Ken, what does this mean to you?" Stabler looked up and simply replied, "Throw deep."

Those two words embodied the action orientation needed to become a star. Throw deep. Take appropriate action. Make it happen.

The question becomes: How do we know what's appropriate? The answer is: If the situation is not working for you almost anything you do is more appropriate. Inaction means no action. And no action means no change from the current course.

How many times have you seen a salesperson become stuck in the rut of only writing letters to potential prospects instead of picking up the phone and calling on new prospects in person?

The management maxim, "If something doesn't change, we're going to end up where we're headed" is applicable here. Are your sales strategies, tactics and habits carrying you in the direction you want? Are they carrying you fast enough? Are they giving you the dollars you want? If not, you've got some change coming.

The sixth functional fantasy is *commitment is the key to excellence.*

Excellence starts with knowing what you want, which leads to how to get there. It's extremely difficult to stay committed to vague abstractions. You need to be able to state specifically what you are committed to. This is best formalized in a mission statement.

Leading companies, such as IBM, not only understand this but operate on it. IBM's basic sales training lasts 15 months. That's more than a year of learning and assimilating the corporate mission statement and its resulting strategies and tactics.

A mission statement not only tells you where you're going, it establishes the basis of figuring out how to get there. Without a mission statement we are often at a loss about why we should perform or not perform certain behaviors.

For example, in yesteryear the railroads were the kings of the transportation industry. They were not only at the top of the heap, they were the heap.

From that perspective it's easy to see how their mission statements revolved around being only in the railroad business rather than in the R. J. Reynolds evolutionary mainstream of the transportation industry. This limited focus of what they were selling kept them from making the logical leap into being the leader in new transportation technologies.

Today trucking, airplanes, water transportation and containerization in combination with these transportation methods have eroded and dissolved the throne on which King Railroad once sat.

On the other hand, neither companies nor individuals can afford to attempt being all things to all people in mission performance.

For example, some time back Merrill Lynch introduced a new ad campaign stating, "Merrill Lynch is bullish on America." You may recall the thundering herds. But that theme somehow didn't make their phones ring to the level they'd hoped. Further focus showed they weren't selling to America at large. They were selling to a particular breed of American investors—ones who took some amount of pride in their investments and individuality. Ones who were not particularly enthralled with being part of the herd. Ones who considered themselves a breed apart. The narrowing of focus paid off very well. Now in their updated campaign they are focusing on this breed's dream, "To know no boundary." We predict success.

There are several important things to know about commitment. One is that commitment is an inside-out proposition. It starts with what is intrinsically important to you and builds from there. In doing so it relates to the work-is-play concept. Commitment starts with what makes us tingle. It also relates to your behaviors because you are responding to your values, beliefs, needs and habits.

A second thing to know about commitment is the less committed you are, the more difficult things seem. The story is told of a neighbor who went to a farmer's house and asked to borrow his rope. The farmer thought about it for a moment and shook his head and said, "Nope, I'm afraid not. I need my rope to tie up my milk." The neighbor looked puzzled. "You don't need rope to tie up milk." The farmer shook his head and said, "Well, I guess the fact is that when you don't want to do something, one excuse is darn near as good as the next." That's the nature of low commitment.

The third point regarding commitment is equally true. The more committed you are to something, the less difficult things seem. The Impressionist artist Renoir in his later years was so debilitated by painful arthritis that every single brush stroke he took gave him excruciating pain. It was so acute that his friend Matisse once asked him why he did it. Renoir replied that the joy he got from the beauty of his creation was far greater than the pain he had to endure.

The next point on commitment is that it can be developed systematically in ourselves and in others. Tennis great Bjorn Borg put it this way in a magazine article some years back. "I don't regret anything in my life. I remember how I used to take the train to Stockholm every day after school to play tennis. All those years I was coming home late, studying, getting up to go to school, getting on the train again. It's gotten results, but even if it hadn't, even if I wasn't able to become a champion, I would still know that I gave it my best shot. I tried. I got on the train and gave it my best." People stay committed to those people, organizations and procedures that they identify with and that they believe give them what they want and need.

Supersalesman Joe Girard's understanding of this is part of what consistently made him the number one retail car salesman in the world. He believes that people buy for emotional reasons, and he therefore make a point of focusing exclusively on his customers' emotional needs. Before ever showing them a car, he ascertained precisely what their inclinations and concerns were. In doing this he assures them they would get what they wanted. Then, after the sale, he continued to reinforce this emotional focus with monthly mailings to his 13,000 current customers. Instead of sending his customers stock brochures of new Chevrolets, he sent greeting cards. The cards differed each month, but the inside message was always the same: I like you.

The seventh and last functional fantasy is *if I give others what they want and need then they will give me what I want and need*. Perhaps you've heard it stated in other ways – "As ye sow, so shall ye reap" or even, "What goes around comes around."

In the world of sales, service and pricing it's easy to slip into believing that money is the only motivator of significance in our business transactions. But people's payoffs come in many forms – only one of which is money.

For example, a colleague of mine was brought into a law firm as a $250-an-hour expert witness. Because of the timing of the case he was asked if he would stop by on Saturday to discuss some of the particulars. He was going to be in the area anyway and mentally categorized the meeting as a goodwill gesture rather than billable time. In the course of the hour-long meeting the lawyer had his secretary bring him a Coca-Cola without offering one to our colleague.

In sharing this story with us he concluded with a smile, "You know, that's the first time I ever encountered a $250 Coca-Cola." What our colleague wanted was appreciation and demonstrated goodwill in that context. What he settled for was $250 for that hour.

On a more positive note, I was scheduling an international conference in Luxembourg and was on a site inspection. It

happened to be over the New Year holiday and the hotel's
dining rooms were filled to overflowing for New Year's Eve. The
assistant manager of the Intercontinental Hotel of Luxembourg realized that the group of six in my party would have
no place to dine or celebrate because of last-minute scheduling
of the trip. When he saw our disappointment, he took it upon
himself, personally, to secure a table for six at his finest
restaurant. This personal attention was largely responsible for
our selecting that hotel for my conference. After all, personal
attention and special service were among our hotel selection
criteria for the conference. This brings us back full circle to
where we began. We start by defining what you want and need
and then dovetail it—matching it—with what your customers
want and need, ideally fitting it all together in an energized
success spiral of helping and winning.

Just for argument's sake, let's take the reverse of all these
functional fantasies and see if they sound familiar. Anything
worth doing is worth doing badly. The opposite is, "If first you
don't succeed then give up." The second, I am responsible for
my own outcomes. The reverse of this would be, "Others are
responsible for my good and bad fortune. I am simply a victim
of circumstance." Third, work is play. The reverse of this would
be, "Work is something we must tolerate until vacation."
Fourth, in every adversity are hidden the seeds of victory. The
reverse would be, "Adversity is nature's signal that you are
about to lose." Fifth, things don't get better by accident but by
appropriate action. The reverse of this would be, "You are either
lucky or you are not lucky. Some are born with it, some aren't."
(By the way, the only people who really say this are those who
are implying that they aren't lucky.) Sixth, commitment is the
key to excellence. The reverse of this is, "Commitment limits me
too much." And last, if I give others what they want and need,
then they will give me what I want and need. The reverse of that
would be, "Only when somebody starts giving me what I want
and need will I help them too."

You've probably noticed by now that the reverse of all the functional fantasies have a familiar ring. Why is that? Because there are more people out making excuses for not winning than enjoying the fruits of victory. The importance of our discussing these functional fantasies before getting into the real meat of the Beyond Selling Program is that frankly some things must be believed to be seen. And most often, whether you believe you can or believe you cannot, you are probably right.

Our brains function somewhat like computers. We are constantly entering data through our five senses – seeing, hearing, feeling, tasting and smelling. The data is stored visually and auditorily in similar fashion to a video recorder. These sounds and images are then stored in our brains for later retrieval.

One of the primary retrieval mechanisms is the use of questions. For example, ask yourself the following question: "What did I have for breakfast this morning?" Did you make a mental photograph or a movie? Did it have sound or not?

Now ask yourself, "What would I like to have the next time I eat?" Notice that your brain responds to this internal question by providing you with visual and/or auditory information. It's almost as if you had pressed the right key on a computer and the data was supplied on your screen automatically.

Since the brain reacts somewhat automatically to questions, can you imagine the impact of bombarding it with such questions as, "Why can't I sell this person?" "What's wrong with my presentation?" "Why do I keep making mistakes?" In all these cases your brain will immediately create words, pictures and even feelings that presuppose negativity and failure. The same can be said for negative affirmations such as, "I can't." When such statements are made the brain will similarly access experiences that reinforce and support these negative affirmations. It, therefore, becomes all too easy for us to fall into habitual patterns which keep us where we are rather than help us move up to the next level.

The alternative is mental rehearsals of your desired out-come—what you want rather than what's getting in your way. In this vein, peak performance researcher Dr. Charles Garfield, in *Peak Performers: The New Heroes of American Business*, notes that peak performers "report a highly developed ability to imprint images of successful actions in the mind. They practice mentally, specific skills and behaviors leading to those out-comes and achievements which they ultimately attain." (p. 146)

Whether we are being positive or negative about our out-comes, our brains provide us with filters and strategies for letting in congruent information and keeping out information that doesn't comfortably fit.

To keep ourselves in line we use selective perceptual filters. The three main filters are selective perception, where we tend to see what we expect to see; selective recall, where we tend to remember based on our own predispositions; and selective exposure, where we consciously decide what we are going to expose ourselves to.

Years ago I lived in a town that (I believed) had the worst drivers in America. They signaled so infrequently that I began to think that turn indicators were optional equipment on new cars. They tailgated as if trying to see the sex of the next automobile. Can you hear the biases that I felt about that town? Factually, the people were very pleasant and most enjoyable, but through my selective perception the traffic was horrendous. So, as I would drive down one of the major thoroughfares, I tended to selectively perceive only those poor drivers. When someone did something such as cut me off and then drive ten miles an hour in front of me I would shriek, "See, that's how they *all* are." Of course, I was oblivious to all the good drivers that had been around me that day.

Then I would selectively recall, remembering last week when a driver did this, and last month when another did that, and would go back literally years to reinforce that belief system. That's selective recall.

The third filter, selective exposure, relates more closely to the quip, "I've read so much about the evils of smoking and drinking that I finally decided to give up reading." Generally, we try not to expose ourselves to evidence that goes against our basic predispositions. Through using these filters we define our environment and we define ourselves. We approach challenges and obstacles with our perceptual filters fully intact, and we unconsciously adjust our behaviors to keep ourselves in line. For example, if you happen to play golf, perhaps you've had a day when you've shot especially well on the front nine. If so, about the 10th hole you may have started saying to yourself, "Wow, I'm playing way over my head. This is not like me." If that happened, your belief system probably started kicking back in, and most likely on the back nine your game started falling apart as if the law of averages had suddenly arrested you on charges of impersonating a golfer.

Self talk such as "this is not like me," and "I am playing way over my head," is a major factor in canceling or slowing forward momentum. In similar fashion, let's say you had a really lousy front nine on the same golf course . At this point you have a choice. You can say, "This is not like me," and when your belief system buys into that you will generally improve your score on the back nine. Or your perceptual filter may be simply saying, "Oh no, I am having another terrible day; screwing up in the first nine guarantees that I am going to screw up all the way through." If that is your belief system you most likely will continue to mess up.

What triggers this response is a mental program in our heads of what "reality" should be. When something alerts us to our reality being off course, our unconscious minds suddenly start working to set things back in order.

If you happen to be a tennis player, you may have had a similar experience. Let's say you are playing someone who is much better than you, yet in the first set you are playing so well you are at the top of your game and you win it 6-2. Then suddenly at the beginning of the second set you too say to yourself, "Wow, I am playing way over my head, this is not like me." Now the player who is better than you is probably also thinking a similar message. "I don't know what's going on but this is not like me. I'd better get back on my game." If indeed those two patterns are flowing in each of your minds, then the next two sets are fairly predictable. You will each follow the direction of your belief system. Your perceptual filters will keep your worlds fully intact, keeping you in your "proper" place.

Now let's apply this to business. A common block we have encountered when observing independent salespeople is a reluctance to move up to calling on larger corporate clients. For example, in the specialty advertising industry we often find qualified, idea-oriented salespeople who have a pattern of selling their promotional ideas and items to mom-and-pop businesses rather than to larger corporate operations that are obviously in a position to purchase much more.

When asked why, these salespeople often respond that they don't feel "ready" to sell to larger companies. This is a common not-like-me pattern that's based on limited self perception and repeated self-talk rather than achievement-based logic.

For example, who is easier to sell, someone who does not have money to spend or someone who does have money to spend? That's right – someone who does have money to spend. Next, who is easier to sell, someone who is spending someone else's hard-earned money or someone spending his own? Right again – someone who is spending someone else's hard-earned money. Now, which is the mom-and-pop business and which is the larger corporate business?

The purpose of this entire *Beyond Selling* program is to learn to pattern your perceptions, thought processes, actions and habits in such a way as to *maximize your business and personal outcomes through fully focused, fully congruent persuasive communication.*

If you will develop the pattern of learning, applying, practicing, and then completing the loop by going back and relearning, reapplying, and repracticing it all, these methods will start enhancing your enjoyment of selling as well as your economic success. You will also notice yourself applying these concepts to your personal life, your relationship with your family and your relationships with your friends.

You will realize that we have a systems approach. It should facilitate all parts of your life as well as all parts of your business. That's why the personal values and integrities side of the program is so important. In the next section, we will introduce you to the fundamental concepts needed for the rest of this book. From there we will develop an *easy-to-use, easy-to-remember* system for approaching selling situations. We will go into great detail with each step and then we will pull all of them together in the end to make them into one cohesive package that you'll be able to tailor to each selling situation you encounter. The adventure has already begun. Let's move forward.

QUESTIONS AND ANSWERS

Question: *Is there a theoretical basis for the ideas you're presenting here?*

Answer: There is a theoretical and practical basis for what's presented here. Much of the theoretical foundation comes from studies on persuasion and influence in the areas of sociology and psychology, as well as from a relatively new area of applied psychology called Neuro-Linguistic Programming (NLP), co-founded by Richard Bandler and John Grinder. The practical, applied part comes from personal experience in professional selling and sales management as well as consulting and sales improvement seminar work with thousands of people nationally and internationally.

Question: *Is this a program to replace what we've been doing in the past?*

Answer: No. It's to enhance your performance and clarify for you which parts of what you are already doing are serving your best interest, and which parts are not. Unless you commonly use hard-sell, coercive manipulation, you'll generally find that what you experience here will not only fit quite neatly into what you already know and do, but will add new dimensions to how well you do it.

Our purpose here is to build on what you are already doing well with specific insights, procedures and examples.

Question: *Do you have to believe in the functional fantasies for your program to work?*

Answer: No. That's why we call them fantasies and not laws. Believe only what you will, and use only what fits you, your needs and your particular situation. If what you are believing and doing are serving you well, by all means stick with them. If they're not, then you may wish to consider other appropriate action.

Our experience is that most highly successful people we have encountered over the years believe in all or most of the seven functional fantasies. Of course, while believing in the functional fantasies is a nice start, it's not enough to assure sales success. That's based more on the actions you take, which is what the rest of this book is about.

CHAPTER TWO

Gaining Rapport

GAINING RAPPORT

Rapport is the foundation upon which all influence is built. You wouldn't consider constructing a large building without first establishing a firm foundation, would you? The same goes for establishing rapport. Everything you are to do in selling and influence is based on your ability to first establish strong consistent rapport in the direction of your desired outcome.

The degree of rapport you establish with a client or a prospect is determined by your ability to pace that prospect. Pacing means getting in rhythm with that prospect on as many levels as possible: getting into the ebb and flow of how that prospect thinks, acts, and processes data.

When you are mirroring that prospect in such a way that you are talking the way he or she talks, sitting the way he or she is sitting, moving in the general patterns that he or she is moving, breathing in the same general rhythms, and appearing to share the same values, you are pacing and thus establishing the basis of rapport.

Many years ago people thought that one either had rapport or didn't have rapport based on some sort of magnetism. Some called it animal magnetism and believed that certain people drew others to them through mystical hypnotic powers.

As with so many old concepts there was a seed of truth in this. But it wasn't magnetism. **It was unconscious or conscious pacing, that is, matching of patterns.**

Let's take a closer look into specific ways of pacing. Since pacing is the initial key to rapport, and rapport is the key to the highest levels of personal influence, let's examine specific ways of pacing.

Think back to the very first time you took a dance lesson. Perhaps it was in junior high school. The dance instructor probably told you that the boy gets to lead and the girl follows. Those were the rules we learned. The male gets to lead and the female follows. I know that in my own situation being the male

I get to lead, and my wife being the female gets to follow. However, I've noticed over the years in dancing with my wife, that whenever we have a situation where she wants to dance in close proximity to another couple, we always end up dancing up in their area. If she wants to dance over close to a window because of a view or a breeze, we always seem to end up there. Yet I'm the one who gets to lead! How can that be? My wife isn't strong enough to physically push me over into the corner where our friends are standing or dancing. Nor would she consider it in her style or her best interest to look at me and say, "Listen, turkey, either you march yourself over there and dance with me in that part of the room or I'm leaving."

But how then? You know how. First she paces me, getting into the rhythm of how I dance. Once she is in that rhythm, she can slowly, subtly, yet definitely with purpose lead me anywhere in the room. And not only am I not aware of it, I enjoy being led.

That's how selling is. First we get in the rhythm of the client. We *dance* with them. We don't use the traditional ways of coercion that trigger fight or flight responses. We don't force, bludgeon, intimidate, or bamboozle them into agreement. Those techniques are passe. Nor do we flock to the flight side and fearfully retreat saying, "If you are not going to play I'm just going to sell someone else." No, there is a third alternative. **It's pacing—getting in the client's rhythm.** And then, once in that rhythm, leading the client.

Studies have shown that a major difference between highly successful salespeople and mediocre salespeople is that mediocre people tend to establish just a small amount of rapport and then move straight into influence strategies. By contrast, highly successful people first build a strong rapport base, and then move into influence strategies. In fact, they establish rapport on several levels before they move to the influencing.

This, however, does not mean they spend an excessively long time building rapport. One can establish a strong rapport base in under three minutes. Rapport is simply pacing on a number of levels. The reason most salespeople do not sell qualified prospects most of the time is because most salespeople operate in their own patterns instead of the prospect's patterns. It is important to know how to pace and how to effectively mirror your prospect's patterns.

EMOTIONAL PACING

In emotional pacing we are trying to meet the client, or prospect, where he or she is emotionally at the moment of our first interaction. Most of the time clients will be somewhat neutral and businesslike. To meet them in their emotional patterns we need to reflect their businesslike demeanor. If they are talking to us in formal tones, we need to respond in formal tones.

Sometimes we meet a client who seems emotionally down. Perhaps you felt this way one day when you were depressed, disappointed, or frustrated. Regardless of what caused it, you felt emotionally down. Now let's pretend that at this moment a salesperson came into *you* to make a sales call. Let's further pretend that this salesperson was bubbly and energetic. "Hello! How are you doin'? Good to see ya! Isn't it a great day today?! Whoa, you look down! What's the matter? Cheer up! The sun's shining, the birds are chirping!"

How would you feel toward that salesperson? You'd probably want to throw him out of the office, or worse. That's why the old glad-hand-hail-and-hearty-how-are-ya-today kind of salesmanship is out. Its effectiveness range usually falls somewhere between ineffective and destructive.

Sure, you want to be upbeat, but don't be so upbeat that you're trying to jitterbug and your customer is barely stumbling along.

Here is another example. Let's say you are feeling delighted, upbeat, cheerful, friendly. Everything is going well and you are feeling on top of the world. You are bursting with delight, and in comes a salesperson who has had a bad day. The salesperson is saying things that you might want to hear, but these things are being said in a beaten emotional tone that suggests, "I'm tired and dragging, so I'm only going through the motions with you." In such a case, you'd probably feel as if that person were dragging you down by attaching negative weights to your emotional high. You'd want to get rid of that salesperson quickly so you could get back to the positive emotion that was upon you.

The point is, if you have a friend, client, spouse, or family member who is emotionally down, respect that. Frankly, you have little choice but to respect it if your intent is to help them to move out of their funk. At the most basic level of pacing you're implying, "I acknowledge you." At another level of pacing the implication is "I understand you." Further up the pacing ladder the implication is "I accept you." Beyond that, the pacing implication evolves to "I like you," "I respect you," and "I trust you." The highest pacing implication, assuming the others have been established, is "I am like you. We're similar."

For example, a friend and client of ours, Matt Matlock, enjoys telling his late father's favorite sales story. His father was a sales superstar, making more than a thousand dollars a week during the depths of the Depression, when twenty dollars a week was considered adequate pay.

He made a cold call to sell some oil drilling equipment to a crusty wildcatter who was reportedly extremely tough on every salesman who ever darkened his door.

As Matt's father entered the office, the wildcatter looked up and, in a menacing growl, demanded, "Well, what the hell can I do for you?"

Without hesitating Matlock growled back, "You can't do a damn thing for me; I've come to do something for you." He left that day with a large order and rapport with a man with whom he shared good business and close friendship until his death decades later.

You might even listen for these cues sometimes when you are talking with a client. Whenever you hear a client or prospect say, "You know, you and I are a lot alike." You've received one of the highest compliments you can get in terms of your rapport-building ability. As you learn pacing skills you are going to find more and more people saying, "Yes, you and I think alike," "We're very similar," or "You understand how I feel." And along with this you'll start noticing improved business relationships resulting in greater mutual profit.

Put yourself in this scenario: What if you make a sales call on a person who is angry, irritated, and perturbed, but not at you? Furthermore, when you come in, he or she says, "Oh no! You're back again. Everything is going wrong today!"

In such a case, your reply would be, in the same tone and tempo, "Oh no! What in the world is happening?" The important thing about emotional rapport is that you are meeting them at the emotion they are displaying. If it's frustration, irritation, or anger, you experience *with* them, *not at* them. That's an important key. Your emotional pacing of frustration or anger at this point needs to be at a situation, not at each other. At that point they may wish to unload a little bit more and you can be appropriately indignant right along with them.

When you are in emotional rapport, it's surprising how often people will share information and insights with you that they never would have in different situations.

For example, I was recently on a flight with my wife to Nassau. As the plane was boarding, one of the attendants was obviously agitated and a bit apprehensive. I guessed it might have been because the airline had cancelled an earlier flight and she was dreading the onslaught of irritated passengers on her now-overbooked flight.

Having preboarded in first class, there were a few moments to chat, so I paced her emotionally and observed, "It looks like we're going to have a planeload of angry people boarding soon."

"Yeah," she sighed. "It's fitting in real well with the kind of day I've been having since I got up."

"Oh no!" I responded in kind, "what happened?"

With that she wove her tale of that day's awful circumstances and ended with this piece of information. "And to top it off, two of the engines on this flight were put on today and have not even been flight tested yet! That's illegal, you know!"

My wife and I could not believe she was risking her job to tell us this. Several minutes later, when the airline made another urgent request for people to give up their seats for another plane and a bonus free trip, my wife and I bid a quick farewell to our new friend, claimed our tickets, and flew out on the *next* flight to Nassau.

Perhaps you've observed political conversations that play through the emotional pacing routine. People who enjoy playing "ain't it awful" will lead with a complaint about the federal government. Then the other person will agree and moan about another governmental irritation. As they commiserate back and forth, they are in near-perfect emotional rapport. And if their outcome is simply to pass the time and enjoy complaining about the federal government, then they will achieve their outcome successfully. If, however, your outcome is to move forward to selling, then meeting them where they are emotionally and using a bridging tactic, such as tying the conversation to the selling situation, will be the best strategy.

To not pace the person is to not establish enough rapport to create or change emotional direction. To reject or contradict directly forces the client to either defend his feelings or mentally dismiss you.

Try this. Put your hands together in front of you and push your right hand against your left hand. Now increase the pressure a little bit and push a little harder. Continue pushing your right hand a little bit harder. And now, harder yet. What is your left hand doing? That's right, it's pushing back. That's the nature of human interaction and thus the power of pacing.

Rather than pushing, and forcing the others to push back (and therefore establishing a battle of wills), we need to pace them, and purposefully shift the momentum to the direction of our outcome with flowing ease rather than brute force.

For example, our friend John recently called on a client—a highly successful restaurateur. The restaurateur was agitated and irritated when John entered. "All I've got is personnel problems. How can you expect me to make a decision to change my brand of beer now?" he challenged.

"Oh no!" John exclaimed, "You've got personnel problems too? We had to let three delivery people go just this month for not showing up!"

This brought about a five minute exchange on how difficult it is "to get good help these days."

When emotional rapport was solid John merely had to mention, "Look, I can see you've got a lot on your mind today, so why don't I just put in a half dozen trial cases and a few promotional pieces and we'll see each other next week to work it all out."

This led to the adoption of John's imported beer later in the month.

By using this strategy, emotional pacing allows you to step into the other person's reality—into his or her world and see, feel and hear things from that perspective. This, in turn, will help you adjust your sales approach to more closely match the client's needs and predispositions. Consequently, the client will more readily accept your reality.

AGREEMENT PACING

Let's relate agreement pacing to an old tried-and-true concept that worked in a hit or miss fashion. You may recall the sales dictum, "Get the client saying 'yes, yes.'" Well, if the client was saying, "Yes, yes, I see, I agree, I understand, I've experienced that before," on *relevant* issues, then indeed the system worked. But if the issues were not relevant to the selling situation, they would *not* produce positive results.

For example, if one said, "Mr. Brown, I see you're wearing a blue suit today, and I notice that you've got a tie pin on and you're wearing new shoes," and on and on like that, "therefore this is going to be a good product," the system obviously wouldn't fly.

Our experience shows that if you tell people a series of seven *relevant* things that they know or believe, the eighth thing you tell them will most often be accepted without question. That's worth repeating and underscoring the key points. Our experience shows that if, in the course of your business conversation, you tell a person *seven relevant* things that he *knows or believes* the *eighth* thing you say *will often be accepted without question.* That's the power of observational pacing, but such pacing must flow naturally and not come across as contrived. This, of course, requires some level of knowing the person you're talking to well enough to know some of the things he knows and believes. Fortunately, if you pay attention, most people give enough information about themselves in one or two meetings for you to be able to list many things they know and believe about their and your business. In doing so, go beyond including just factors; pay special attention to indications of their personal philosophies regarding cost, value, trust, problems, opportunities, human nature and risk taking. The importance of this will become even clearer when we get to values and beliefs pacing later in this chapter.

An example of agreement pacing in the context of strangers coming into a store would be to walk up to a couple looking at stereo equipment and say, "I notice you've been looking at our stereo sets," and wait for them to reply. By stepping into their reality they are not going to say, "No, we weren't looking at your stereo sets." Yet they could easily say "no" to your prematurely asking, "May I help you?" The point of waiting for a reply is that they will tell you where you need to go from there. If they reply, "Yes, we are just browsing," you should say, "Good." Meet them where they are. Agree with them and add, "Please feel free to browse, and please let me know when I might help you in any way." Then retreat. Make sure you stay available by making eye contact or looking over toward them should they give any interest signals that tell you to move back.

If they give no signals but stay a little longer, then you move and say, "I see you are still enjoying browsing. Are you familiar with how our systems sound?" Or, "How do these compare with what you've looked at already?" You'll notice that either of these directions will lead to their disclosing more information about their experiences, thoughts and opinions. Again, this is much better than coming up and asking the rejection question, "May I help you?" to which the answer, most of the time, (unless they are truly ready to make a buying decision) will be "NO." In those situations there is little chance of moving them from lukewarm to hot.

Notice we keep talking about being relevant to your sales or influence outcome in establishing agreement or emotional pacing strategies. Rapport is contextual. You can have rapport in some contexts and not others. Let's combine, for example, emotional and agreement rapport. Imagine you are at a sports event and you are rooting for your favorite team. The people sitting next to you are totally different from you. They are dressed differently, they speak differently, they are of a different social class. Yet they are cheering, observing, and appreciating the exact moves, plays, and strategies you are. Unless they transgress some of your most closely held values, even if they are completely different from you, in the context of that sporting activity you will have rapport. That does not mean that they will be able to turn around and sell you an insurance policy.

Likes like likes. We like people who are like us. We identify with them. We drive the same styles of cars, we belong to the same clubs, we watch the same television programs, we enjoy the same types of music. When people enjoy the things we like, there is a good foundation for rapport. But rapport is more than simply liking. You will recall that rapport includes acknowledging, understanding, accepting, liking, respecting and trusting.

POSTURE PACING

Posture pacing can be thought of as body language pacing. As you continually observe in public the varying levels of posture rapport, you'll become a true appreciator of the power of this particular pacing style.

Imagine two friends sitting across from each other at a small table in a restaurant talking with each other at an incredibly high interest level. Can you picture how their bodies looked? They tend to maintain eye contact, they nod simultaneously, their heads move in a similar pattern, their shoulders are at approximately the same angle and perhaps their legs are crossed in a similar pattern. Even their arms seem to be mirroring each other's arms.

You've seen it before and you've probably noticed it. You also can notice such physical patterning in corporate boardrooms. Very often the body language of the CEO at the head of the conference table will be consciously or unconsciously followed by all at the table. The folded hands in front waiting for the last couple of people to come in may be reflected up and down the table. The stern expression, the erect shoulders, the looking from one side to the other may all be seen in those who are paying close attention to the boss.

Much of posture rapport is done from the chin up. When the client telling you something squints the eyes and furrows the brow, you squint your eye and furrow your brow in response. The friend shakes her head in telling you a woeful story and you find your head shaking in response to how it must have felt. Or the other person laughs a hah-hah laugh with head thrown back and you find yourself laughing aloud too. If they laughingly slap their knee, you may laughingly slap your knee or clap your hands together or tap a desk. Posture rapport is not exactly mirroring, as in having the other person do exactly the same thing in a mirror-like fashion. And it's certainly not a monkey-see-monkey-do situation. It's getting in such rapport that while you'll initially do it consciously, with practice you will soon naturally mirror the person to the degree that you will be in physical harmony with that person.

That does not mean that if the person has a twitch you are going to start twitching also. That does not mean if the person has a funny habit such as scratching the top of his head, or sticking his pinkie finger in his ear, that you are going to scratch the top of your head or stick your pinkie finger in your ear in mirroring fashion.

But there is indeed something that is done physically that acknowledges this to others on their unconscious level. It's called cross-over mirroring. Let's say a person has a strange habit of scratching the top of his head while thinking. Rather than reaching up and scratching the top of your head, you may (as if unconsciously) reach down and scratch the top of your knee, or even rub the top of your knee. The key is to be *inobvious,* but to pattern similarly to their movement. If the prospect has a habit of sticking his pinkie finger in his ear and wiggling it back and forth vigorously, then you may find yourself projecting a similar pattern by reaching down and scratching your sock, or reaching over and scratching the back of your neck slightly, thus matching their pattern. This seems rather laughable in some contexts as you imagine yourself moving, squirming and twitching, but you won't do it a hundred percent. You can't do it a hundred percent. Somewhere around the 50 to 80 percent level of movement will be helpful— especially in facial expression, shoulder posture and head nods.

In a boardroom context people in close alliance will often sit in similar fashion, and those who are not will sit in different fashion. You can sometimes watch the informal body language of how someone pays attention, how he or she nods in unison with the person presenting, or does not nod in unison with the person presenting. Those cues can tell you whether or not they are in rapport.

These are not mind reading skills, however. They simply give hints as to the rapport level at that moment. Rapport is never acted out in a vacuum. It is tied in with what is being discussed, the values being shared, the emotional level, etc.

A while back, I had an opportunity to practice just posture, and a small amount of emotional rapport, without any verbal interaction whatsoever. I was working with a major plastics manufacturer in terms of motivating its sales force. As part of the background work I was riding with salespeople in the field. In this context I was strictly an outside observer of the sales calls that this person was making. It was not my intent or my outcome to say anything to help or hurt the selling situation. I was simply there to observe, to give a critique afterwards, and weave my findings into other motivational and skill-building points for the entire sales organization.

On one particular day, the salesman and I made a trouble-shooting call on a plastics molder who was very dissatisfied. From his perspective he had received a bad batch of raw plastic. From the plastics manufacturer's perspective he had not followed the technical instructions to make it work. Regardless of who was right, when we walked into his plant we found an agitated, hostile, crusty old individualist who felt he had been wronged, and he was hungry for retribution. I was introduced as a company executive who was simply coming along to observe what the salesperson was doing that day. I was not introduced as an outside consultant, so from the molder's standpoint I was part of the company he was so angry with.

The molder's interaction with the sales person was vehement as he shot volley after volley of demands, icy stares, and labored sighs. Without uttering a word I paced him; when he furrowed his brow, clenched his teeth, and fired a question at my sales friend. I mirrored that behavior and looked over and glared at my sales friend in a very similar manner. When the molder heard the response and leaned back with folded arms, I eased into that position myself. In the course of the sales presentation, the molder started to ease his position. He clenched his jaw less, he even smiled once or twice. And as he unclenched his jaw, I did too. As he tentatively smiled, I did too.

We never directly looked at each other doing these things during that time, but the rhythm was definite. I didn't want to be obvious that I was mirroring him, and he may not have consciously noted that I was. There was no acknowledgement whatsoever that I was pacing emotions and mirroring his gestures. After about forty-five minutes we were standing in the lobby saying good bye and he had lapsed back into his original crusty bastard posture and said to the salesperson, "And listen, if you don't live up to the agreement that we have right now, and if you don't get back to me in two weeks with a satisfactory answer, I am going to have your hide, and I am never going to give you another nickel of business again." At that moment he turned to me and gave me an insider's wink as if to say, "You and I know how this game is played."

Through nothing but posture and to some degree emotional rapport, he and I had established a bond through the pacing strategy. It appeared by his wink at the end; while he was giving the salesman a very hard time, he and I knew what the real outcome would probably be. And I was on his side, even though I had been introduced as a member of the other organization.

You may be with familiar with the fact that different parts of the country often have different types of posture rapport. There are some cultures within the United States, for example, where people don't look each other right in the eye when they talk. I have been in selling situations in the rural south where the two of us didn't seem to talk directly to each other, but to a spot on the ground that both of us stared at, while exchanging conversation. In those situations, had I looked up from that spot and tried to make direct eye contact, it would have broken the rapport. It would have established a communication barrier. Ease of communication would have disappeared.

Posture rapport is very important, whether it's matching eye contact, sitting position, or even breathing.

Matching breathing directly is difficult. If a person is expressing frustration, you will often hear a big sigh. While you recognize that sigh as an expression of emotion, you are not always sure of the level of frustration or whether it's aimed at you, at the sales situation, or at something else. But breathing rapport strategies suggest that the heave of the chest and letting out of the air should to some degree be followed by you. "I feel as you feel. I understand. You and I are alike," is the message that comes across.

Let's take another situation. Perhaps if you have taken body language courses or read books about what varying positions mean, you have burdened yourself with the task of interpreting body language quite as if it's a language like Spanish, French, or German. Frankly, it's not a language like Spanish, French, or German. One cannot read another person like a book. One can, however, get very good cues. Problems arise when we start interpreting. For example, most people have heard that when a person sits with his arms and legs crossed it's a sign of resistance.

It *may* be a sign of resistance, or it may be a sign that the person is a little bit chilly or cold. It could mean that person enjoys folding his arms because it stretches his back. Maybe he's feeling fat that day. When some people feel that their stomach is pooching out a little bit too much, they tend to sit with their arms folded. Maybe they are very receptive to what you have to say but they are not comfortable about how they are dressed. The point is, *we don't know what the body posture means.* All we know is what we can see. Anything beyond that is only a guess. And when we guess we're in danger of going off on a misdirected tangent. Pacing saves us from such misdirections.

If a prospect sits and talks with his arms and legs crossed, he may indeed be resisting. If so, the absolute worst thing that you can do is try to break through that barrier by leaning forward and becoming all the more adamant, vehement, enthusiastic, or charming. What will he do? He will do what your left hand did earlier in this chapter. He'll resist more. So, assuming that the initial reading of resistance was correct, breaking physical rapport by pushing forward when he closes up is the worst strategy to use. He'll simply close up even tighter. But by pacing and mirroring you will naturally back off and discuss your plan with your legs crossed and your arms crossed as if even you need protection from such fast-moving challenges. That physical rapport approach allows your client to loosen up and become less defensive.

Let's now assume his "closed" body language is because he simply enjoys sitting that way occasionally. As before, you act the same way. The same posture rapport is established and therefore you have another level of identification; the two of you enjoy sitting that way together.

Let's assume your client is uncomfortable about the way he looks, and he is afraid that you are sitting there judging him. Again, you sit in a way very similar to his. Probably not consciously, but unconsciously, he will tend to relax a little bit more because your nonverbal behavior is neither aggressive nor judgmental. You have commonality.

You've known these things instinctively for some time. For example, when there is a little child in the room and you want to establish rapport, do you stand tall over the child and look down, or do you get at the child's level and start talking to that child? If an infant is giggling, cooing and laughing, and you want to delight in that child's moment, do you find yourself talking goo-goo-gah-gah baby talk and making funny little faces? Of course you do. You meet the child where he is.

When a toddler is crying, have you ever found yourself getting down to that level and making a sad little pouty face as you held out your arms? Sure you have.

Here's how far this natural inclination to pace can go. There is a small bar in Indian Rocks Beach, Florida called P. J.'s. It's named for a colorful parrot who sits perched in a large cage at the end of the bar.

P.J. is normally quite taciturn, but when he speaks (as the saying goes) people listen. In fact, they do more than listen. They immediately involve themselves in getting P. J. to speak more. How? You guessed it. It's not uncommon to find several patrons squawking and talking like a parrot to encourage more parrot talk from P.J. And yes, P. J. responds.

You see, when you're interacting with an infant, a small child, or even a parrot, you're operating much closer to an instinctive level. By the time we start interacting with clients we start game playing. We start adding misdirection plays. We start covering up the real feelings. We start misforming reality.

How important is posture rapport? We suspect it's not an accident that in the military it is required that subordinates must get in step with a higher ranking officer when simply walking across a military post or a base.

Perhaps the epitome of posture rapport is dancing. Probably, in your own experience, you found a relationship starting to bloom and emotions starting to stir in the context of dancing with someone. There is something very appealing—even seductive—about moving one's body in harmony with another person's body. It's certainly no accident that some fundamentalist religions find this physical pacing seductive to the point of being threatening to them. Therefore many strict fundamentalists are against dancing for reasons relating to its ability to influence people into disapproved behaviors.

In sporting events physical pacing and emotional rapport are regularly orchestrated by cheerleaders and bands. Through well-rehearsed cheers, chants, clapping and gesturing in unison, the excitement and enjoyment of the game escalate, surge and resurge, affecting spectators and players alike in an upward emotional spiral.

Cheering also involves tone and tempo rapport.

TONE AND TEMPO PACING

The tone and tempo of your voice are yet another level of pacing that can establish rapport. The tone and tempo are *how* you speak. It's not what you say, but how you say it. It's the speed, loudness, inflection, and rhythm. Regardless of your words, your tone and tempo are auditory fingerprints of who you are and how you're expressing yourself at that moment.

Each of us tends to speak at the pace that we *enjoy* listening. The rate of speed varies among individuals and even among speech communities.

If you happen to be from the Northeast (let's say New York City) you have possibly spoken to people from the Deep South and felt that you could grow old and die before they finished their sentences. You perhaps found yourself unconsciously, or physically, finishing sentences for them, and wishing they would hurry up.

If you happen to be from the Deep South, (let's say Biloxi, Mississippi) you perhaps have cringed in discomfort at what felt like brusqueness, lack of empathy, lack of savoring the moment in the conversation, or even rudeness when you spoke with people from the North. Similar discomfort can be felt in any patterning that goes against the tone and tempo at which we like to listen.

When pacing tone and tempo, it's especially important to realize you are not imitating the other person's accent. It would be offensive to most Southerners to have someone with a New York accent mimic their accent in order to try to build rapport. In similar fashion, a person from the Deep South is not likely to be a successful rapport builder by mimicking a New York accent. However, you can move toward that person's tone and tempo. As you get better at it, rapport will increase. The movement should occur so naturally that neither you nor the other person realizes you have moved into his or her way of speaking. In a sense, this is a vocal chameleon effect. A good communicator will change without even thinking about it. The pace at which he or she speaks adjusts after only a few words with another person.

Is this a natural pattern? Yes, definitely. European children who fluently speak several languages make this shift automatically. In response to foreigners they can switch languages and hardly realize they are doing it. What is even more interesting is that if questioned later about which language they spoke, the children often will have no idea which language it was because they so naturally move from one language to the next.

In contrast, when faced with a foreigner who does not speak our language, we Americans will sometimes try to communicate by increasing the volume and tone of urgency of our words. We have witnessed American tourists in Europe emphatically shouting the word "bathroom" in a vain attempt at better communication. One naive soul we saw even tried spelling it.

If you are having some doubts about how well tone and tempo pacing might work, you're similar to participants in one of my seminars recently. When I made these points in a group of about thirty people, a Latin fellow named Joe spoke up. In his Latino tone and tempo he took exception. "Just a moment," he said in a staccato pattern.

"Yeah, Joe," I replied. "What is it?" in the same pattern.

"Are you telling me that if I talked in a pattern the way other people talk, they're not going to know I am doing it?"

"That's right, Joe. If you talk the way they talk, they're not going to know you are doing it," I responded in his same staccato pattern.

At that moment a fellow from the Deep South, whose name was Ralph, started laughing out loud. I turned to Ralph, and, knowing how he spoke, said , "What is it, Ralph?" using his slow Southern pattern.

"Why, he doesn't even know you're doin' it to him, does he?" he drawled.

"Nope Ralph," I said as close to Ralph's drawl as I could get. "He doesn't even know it, does he?"

At this point Joe started laughing. Joe realized that Ralph could tell the difference when I was speaking to him, but Ralph had not heard the difference when I was using Ralph's own pattern. The point is that if we pace well without mimicking, but match as closely as possible the tone and tempo of the person we are talking with, we will greatly enhance rapport. An easy example in normal conversation is the way some people speak in hushed tones. They are low key, with almost a funeral parlor ambience to the words they say. If you speak to such a person with bright, upbeat, bouncing tones, then you are going to break rapport. On the other hand, some people enjoy talking in bubbly fashion. Balloons, streamers, and butterflies seem to come from every bouncy word they share. Those people enjoy being spoken to in that same tone and tempo, with bounce, verve and delight.

Can you recall the discomfort you've felt when you whispered something in a hushed tone to someone and they shot back with a loud "What?" Or perhaps you can recall a situation where everyone was speaking in a quiet, somber tone and one person's voice tended to carry much farther than the others, making the perpetrator seem out of place. You can also probably recall a time when you and some friends were having a lively discussion in a fast-paced manner and someone started talking in a much slower, droning fashion that seemed to break the rhythm of the moment. If you can recall feeling discomfort in any of these situations, then your intuition already knows the importance of pacing through tone and tempo.

LANGUAGE PACING

Language pacing has two major components. One is form and the other is patterning. Form includes organizational and professional buzzwords. These buzzwords are often cues to let the other person know that the user has read the latest article, the latest book, or has talked to people who are in the know. The importance of these buzzwords is in establishing identification of who is in tune and who is not. Therefore, using the appropriate buzzwords and listening and clarifying when you're not familiar with one is very important. Now here is an interesting dilemma. If someone uses a buzz word that you don't know, should you stop them for clarification? The answer is yes. The safe way of doing this is to say, "When you use the term 'appropriate corporate culture,' what do you mean specifically?" By phrasing it that way you learn and leave open the possibility that you are merely probing his or her particular interpretation. That can also get you sensory-specific answers—i. e., those that are observable and describable in terms of the five senses.

Assuming you know the general concepts in the arena that you're working, there will be very few of these buzzwords that you cannot figure out in context. When you're certain you understand it, be sure to feed your newly learned word back to the other person. If you're not certain, or haven't a clue what the buzzword means, ask directly, with confidence. It will enhance your credibility and knowledge, and you'll be able to use your new words in the future with many others.

Pacing how words are used can be an extremely powerful rapport builder. Or, if not done correctly, it can be an extremely powerful rapport breaker.

The other component of language pacing is putting your words into the other person's thinking and speaking pattern. This is a lot easier than it may seem. Since we tend to operate in patterns, we tend to think and speak in patterns. These patterns are typically visual, auditory and kinesthetic, and olfactory/gustatory. The first, and certainly most common, is the visual mode. Our language is full of such examples. If you can *see* what we are saying, you will get a *clear perspective* and we'll share the same *viewpoint.* See what we mean?

Visually oriented people want you to *focus* so you *see* situations *insightfully.* They want you to observe their *bright* ideas and *colorful visions.* They want you to have a *clear overview* because, to them, *seeing* is believing.

While we all use all four of the processing modes to some degree, the second most common pattern that we use is the auditory mode. You hear the auditory mode when people are telling you, "*Listen* to what I am *telling* you," "I *hear* what you are *saying,*" and "Let's *discuss* this till it *sounds* right."

These people pay special attention to *keeping their ears open* for what *rings* true. Your well-chosen words are usually *clear as a bell* to these people.

The third most common verbal pattern is kinesthetic. Kinesthetic people *process* most comfortably with *feeling* words. Their words may *soothe* you or *rub* you the wrong way. When you *grasp* what they *share,* they *feel happy.* Ideas *hit* them and they have *gut feelings.* They hope you'll *keep in touch.*

The fourth and least common verbal pattern is olfactory/gustatory—smelling and tasting. These people will speak of *sniffing out* opportunities, or giving someone a *taste* of his own medicine. When business is bad it *stinks*—possibly because of *rotten* luck—which, of course, they find *distasteful.*

When a person leans toward one particular verbal pattern, you need to respond back in that particular style of wording. This is important because he or she is using that pattern to process thoughts and thus create his or her individualized reality. For example, another couple was visiting us at our home recently. This couple had had some very good financial success over the years, and the husband was enjoying talking about the new Mercedes they had just bought. As he talked about how it looked and how it fit his image, the wife fidgeted a bit and then spoke poignantly.

"You know," she said, "things are going very well now, and we have acquired so many nice things. Even so, sometimes I feel that things just aren't as smooth as they used to be."

This evidently hit an old sensitive spot for him, for it set him off immediately. "She just can't see the forest through the trees," he interrupted. "All she has to do is look around her and see how much I care."

"I know", she countered, "but sometimes it just doesn't feel like it used to feel. Somehow, I just can't put my finger on it, but it's..."

He interrupted again, feeling somewhat defensive (I would guess). "Look at how I show I care—the jewelry I buy her, the house, the cars. If she can't see that I love her from all of that, she's gotta be blind."

The wife was so classically kinesthetic in her orientation and her husband was so classically visual, that I couldn't help but probe a little farther and asked her, "What would it take to make you *feel* really good—the way it used to feel?" She thought a moment, her shoulders squirmed a bit, and she smiled as if in a reverie and said, "I'd enjoy if we held hands more... if he touched me more in public... if maybe when we we're sitting in a movie he would put his arm around me." The smile and the dream-like look in her eyes were certainly congruent with what she was saying, as she reported what would feel good to her.

"Could you *see* yourself doing that?" I asked, turning to the husband. He defocused his eyes as if imagining it, and said, "Sure I could see myself doing that."

I turned back to her. "How would that make you feel?"

"Wonderful!" she said.

My intent was polite conversation, not marriage counseling, so I simply posed the suggestion to him. "I think her perspective might be cleared up with more hugs and touching."

"That would really feel nice," she added, and we changed the conversation to matters less personal.

Not only were they communicating in two completely different languages (she in what would "feel right" to her, and he
with what "looked right"), but the difference was also reflective
of what they valued. Her highly valued criteria were not centered around the pretty things, though she certainly liked them
and appreciated them. What she valued most highly was what
was reflected in her language. It was the touching and the
feeling of togetherness that she held dear.

He, being quite image oriented, was much more dazzled by
how things appeared, how new presents shined and how good
they, as a couple, looked together. While they both most probably loved each other equally, they demonstrated and experienced love differently. There was no good pattern or bad pattern
here, only different patterns.

This certainly is not to say that people do not vary from
their patterns. They certainly do (some more than others). But
there are still common threads throughout. Responding to a
person in the pattern he or she is using at that moment can be
the difference between matched or mismatched communication
styles.

By way of review, we've noted that people think primarily
(but not exclusively) in either visual, auditory, kinesthetic or
olfactory/gustatory terms. Perhaps this is a good time for you
to take an inventory of your dominant language/thinking
pattern.

Are you primarily visual? Do you tend to see pictures in
your mind? Do you often run a movie in your mind about events
that have happened or might occur? Can you easily visualize
how things should or might be? If so, you'll probably see that
your language reflects this clear perspective as you look back at
recent conversations.

Or perhaps you are primarily auditory. Do you most easily
remember events by hearing a conversation inside your head?
Do you hear your voice and the other person's voice, or perhaps
your voice playing both sides of the conversation? Do you find

your thought patterns being interrupted by sounds that other people seem to ignore? If so, you can tell by these suggestions that your language and thought processing patterns are primarily auditory, because the examples you've read here sound right.

Or you may feel you're kinesthetic. Do you find you make decisions by how the situation feels to you? Do you often recall things by going through the physical motions? If you lose your keys do you have to retrace your steps and feel various objects in order to get in touch with where you left them? If so you already have the strong sense that you're kinesthetic because your grasp of reality feels so right.

Here in the United States, olfactory and gustatory processing systems are not favorites. In fact, much of our advertising is aimed at getting rid of odors. In other countries we find some languages are much richer in that they have words for smells and tastes that make many distinctions that do not even exist in our language. However, both smell and taste can be powerful stimuli, as has been noted in a recent real estate sales course where salespeople were instructed to have chocolate chip cookies baking in the oven when holding an open house.

If you are principally olfactory/gustatory you notice that you mentally reconstruct events by recalling tastes and smells associated with those moments. Or perhaps you recall unpleasant events and get a bad taste in your mouth. Or, as you recall specific meals you've had, you can easily remember the tastes and smells of the various foods on the table. If so, you are tasting life's banquet as an olfactory/gustatory person.

Now let's consider three sports cars – one of which you will buy.

The first car is shiny and has a sleek European flair. It's extremely attractive without being overly flashy. You can see its aerodynamic nature through the slant of the hood and its raised trunk. Its interior and exterior are color coordinated. Its top folds down and is covered by a self-sealing metal plate so

there is no unsightly hump. When you imagine yourself driving
in this car on a spring day with the top down, you can see the
admiring stares as people turn to appreciate the look of quality
in car and driver.

As the door shuts in the second car you can hear the
resonance of its solidness. As you fire the engine and rev the car
in neutral you can hear the awesome power lying just below the
hood flowing through the baffles in the muffler. You can imagine yourself driving down a highway hearing the full quality of
the ten speakers playing your favorite stereo music, all enhanced by the sound of the word and the purr of the engine,
knowing that by merely shifting the gear the engine will
scream forth, reverberating with sounds of excitement.

To sit in car three is to be cradled in luxury. The seats are
contoured to your body. The leather is smooth and pliable,
inviting you to touch it and appreciate the quality. The dash-
board is appointed with fine woods, sanded and varnished to
the utmost smoothness. As you turn the engine over and pull
out onto the street, you can feel a surge of power and sense the
speed and safety. As you accelerate and make your first turn,
you feel the car's wheels grabbing the road and have the sense
of the car and driver being one.

Which of the three appeals to you the most? Which would
you probably choose?

If you're highly visual, chances are the first car looks best
to you. If you're highly auditory, chances are the second car
sounds like a better choice. And if you're highly kinesthetic,
chances are you're itching to get your hands on the third car.

The fact is that all three descriptions were of the same car.
They just accentuated different positives as appreciated by
people with visual, auditory or kinesthetic patterns.

Therefore, in situations where you are dealing with a client
who is extremely visual, you need to understand that seeing is
believing to that person. You'll want to show him how it looks.

You want to speak in visual words to show a clear perspective on the total picture.

If the person is auditory, you want to talk to her in terms of what sounds logical and what she may be asking herself. She may want to talk your idea over with some other people or think aloud. You may offer to discuss the details until you're perfectly in tune.

When selling to a person who is basically kinesthetic, you'll want to talk about getting a feel for it, grasping the key points, and moving in a good direction.

When selling someone who uses primarily the olfactory/gustatory mode, you want to give her a plan she can sink her teeth into. Let her chew over the facts, sniff out the problems, and come up with a very tasty solution for everybody.

When in doubt, or when speaking to a group, you should mix or combine your patterns with a leaning toward the visual. Most people operate primarily in a visual mode. In fact, in my experience three out of four people in this country are primarily visual, with many of those combining visual with another mode in their speech patterns. They combine visual and auditory in such expressions as, "I think you can *see what I am saying here.*" If you use combinations like that and other combinations such as *hearing* the proof and *feeling* secure, or *touching* all the points to make that *clear*, it will tend to keep you on safe middle ground.

Additionally, beyond the sensory-based verbs we've been discussing there are also a number of predicates that are *unspecified* in sensory-based terms. Verbs like understand, remember, consider, know, believe, change, give, and think (to mention a few) are like wild cards. They fit in any of the patterns because of their general, unspecified nature.

In summary, the best way to handle ambiguous situations is to simply pace your audience, whether it's one or several people, and respond in the same frame that they are responding in to you. For example, if a client says at a group meeting, "I really don't see what you are getting at here," say, "Let me put it in a clearer perspective. Look at it this way."

If another person says, "Yeah, but it still doesn't sound right," then you'd say, "I hear what you're saying. Which part doesn't sound totally right yet?" The point is to simply respond in the same language in which the person has posed the objection, the question, or the viewpoint. When in doubt use predicate combinations and unspecified predicates as explained above.

In order to fully understand the power of predicate pattern matching, try the following experiment: Find an innocuous situation, such as having a conversation in a coffee shop or an airport with someone you don't know very well. Identify the primary pattern the person is using – visual, auditory or kinesthetic – and deliberately mismatch his or her predicates. If he or she is using visual, you use only auditory and kinesthetic. If he or she is using auditory, you use only visual and kinesthetic, etc. In doing so, notice how quickly rapport breaks down. When you come to appreciate how this works in this low-involvement, low-payoff situation, you'll more fully appreciate the importance and power of matching and mismatching predicates in high-involvement, high-payoff situations, such as selling and relationship management.

VALUES AND BELIEFS PACING

Values and beliefs pacing means that you do not step on the other person's values and beliefs. The more highly valued the other person's beliefs or values are, the more important it is not to trounce on them. Stated another way, "Be careful not to ever blow your nose on someone else's flag."

In some selling situations, this can be difficult because sometimes we call on people who have completely different values than what we have. Sometimes we call on people whose values are so diametrically opposed that we have to come back to our own values and question whether we want to do business with them.

Here we are only interested in those people we want to do business with, and therefore it's in our best interest to have some level of rapport based on values and beliefs in addition to the other levels of rapport. Is values and beliefs rapport important? Let's pretend that you invite a business acquaintance over to your home for dinner. In doing this, you are serving an extraordinary pasta with clam sauce dish for that dinner. Let's further pretend that this is one of your favorite recipes and you're very, very proud of it. When your guest arrives, you get ready to serve the dinner and he says, "I'm really sorry, I don't care for seafood of any kind. But, go ahead and eat, I'm truly not hungry."

How do you feel at that point? If you are angry, sad, or embarrassed, you can certainly realize that rapport is not at a particularly high level at that point.

Let's say someone comes over to your house and she's looking at your bookshelf and turns to you and says, "I notice you don't have any current bestsellers." And you, indeed, don't. So the implication is that she would expect you to have them, and here you don't. How do you feel toward that person—in high rapport or low rapport?

Fortunately, it is possible to have good conversations and good business dealings and good relationships with people who hold beliefs that are very different from our own. Thank goodness this is true, or else there would never be any possibility of cultural harmony on the face of this globe.

That said, to enhance pacing and rapport at this level we need to establish what we call *agreement frames*. The major one of these is an *agreement caricature*. Just as a caricature of someone's face highlights certain elements and de-emphasizes others, agreement caricatures also highlight and de-emphasize various points simultaneously. With agreement caricatures we emphasize or highlight the points of agreement and de-emphasize or ignore the points that are not relevant to our agreement frame.

Recently a client approached me with the problem that one of his key salesmen's productivity on the road had suddenly diminished. In working with the salesman, I was told he was seriously contemplating divorce and was not focused enough to continue to put together his highly complex proposals. On further talking with him it became apparent that what was tearing him up was that he was very much in love with his wife and had a strong belief in a monogamous marriage. But he was becoming tempted.

It also became apparent that he was using the agreement caricature backwards! What he was doing was meeting many professional businesswomen on the road and asking himself, "What does this woman have that my wife does not have?" After a week of being on the road and having asked himself that question many times he had a long list of attributes that his wife did not have. Consequently, he developed an ever-increasing negative feeling about her.

The key to success with him was helping him to change his frame of reference. Instead of asking himself the question, "What does this woman have that my wife doesn't?" he began to ask the question, "What does my wife have that this woman doesn't?" By asking this new question he began to develop a long list of positive attributes that his wife had that other women didn't, and thus he began to rebuild his very strong positive feelings about her. (This example could easily have been reversed with a woman on the road comparing her husband to the businessmen she met.)

As you can see, the agreement caricature is an important vehicle to utilize in developing belief and value rapport. But the question regarding what is to be highlighted in the caricature must be something that focuses on agreement and harmony.

Do you have any clients who you approach and find yourself building a case out of what you don't like about them? If so, have you noticed how easily that negative caricature builds – even to the point of inhibiting good communication and good business? If so, try turning it around and building on what is good, redeeming and worth appreciating. Granted, the turn-around is not often easy, but it is worth it. Beyond turning our agreement caricature to the positive there are other useful strategies. For example, in many cases we can agree with someone's intent without agreeing with his methods. Similarly, we can agree with some people's approval-seeking needs, yet not agree with their approval-seeking behavior.

In values and beliefs rapport you can use all of the pacing levels: I acknowledge you, I understand you, I accept you, I like you, I respect you, and I am like you. For example, if your client is angry and you are not sure it is justified, you can with all integrity say, "I certainly respect your feelings on this." Having said that, the next word that follows should absolutely *not* be the word "but."

For many, especially in confrontive situations, or where two sides are defending values or beliefs, the word "but" negates everything in front of it. At best, it makes what came before it seem like a well placed setup. For example, "I really like the outfit you are wearing, but yellow is simply not your color." With that wording the value of the dress is much more diminished than if the person were to say, "I really like your outfit, *and*, if it were some other color besides yellow, I would even like it more." In both of those approaches the person expressed some disapproval about the color yellow. However, in the second it is softened much more by the agreement frame 'and' rather than the 'but.' Other examples would be, "I respect that viewpoint and I am certain that you can also see mine."

The best way to establish and maintain values rapport is to not take exception. Since the business world simply doesn't work that way, I suggest that when you must take exception to something, do it without losing undue momentum.

CULTURAL PACING

Corporate Culture Pacing

Cultural pacing is a broad, overarching, catchall for pacing the varying aspects within the organization you are calling on. Very often, regardless of how the person acts and thinks off the job, the decision making process he or she uses at work will be greatly affected by how the corporate culture dictates that success is achieved. For example, most business people do not wear the same style clothes off the job as they do on the job. For most of us, protocols such as how we interact with other people are not identical on the job and off the job, though we can all think of examples of people who have incredibly high amounts of crossover from one to the other. Images that come to mind may be the military officer whose family life mirrors the strict protocols of his military environment.

In looking at cultural rapport, we need to pace on several different levels that are somewhat diverse. Consider dress within the organization. You've noticed that some organizations are pinstriped with white shirts while some are open collar. Some organizations lean toward double-knit suits and others toward wool blends. While there are many good books on dressing for success and how to interact well in corporate America, it's worth noting that dress codes not only vary among different regions of the country, but also from business to business within any given region. And while the pinstriped suit is normally considered appropriate in corporate America, the same organization that applauds it at one level may reject it at another. For example, imagine trying to establish rapport with workers on an assembly line. Place yourself on that assembly line wearing a Hickey-Freeman pinstriped suit, white shirt, conservative tie, Gucci shoes and a leather briefcase. How much rapport are you going to be able to develop on that assembly line? Would they confide their needs, concerns and predispositions to you?

This, however, isn't to recommend that you dress exactly like the people on the assembly line if you are working with them as a manager trying to establish rapport and develop ways to streamline their operation.

The way you would want to dress would be how they'd expect you to dress in that role with them. On that same assembly line, for example, hard-hats, safety glasses, a white shirt rolled up partially and no tie would probably be acceptable, if indeed you were a representative of management coming to learn and solve problems. It's a matter of context. The chances are that if you try to match exactly in the assembly line with what the people were wearing, you would look about as well matched as someone on his first day at a dude ranch trying to fit in with the other cowboys.

By the way, the late (and infamous) Jimmy Hoffa—an extremely powerful influencer of his time and circumstance— often wore expensive suits without alienating his rank-and-file power base. How? One cultural pacing tool he used was his choice of socks—white socks.

The uniform that relates to who you are in the task you are performing is so important in a pacing sense because it provides others a shortcut for knowing who you are and what you are about. They don't have to spend the time, the energy, or the effort to categorize or analyze what to expect.

It also frees them from doing comparisons between you and the other people who have come through in a similar role. How we dress is so symbolic of who we are that many people accept it in predigested fashion without any question at all. Consider how many thieves have discovered this. They realize that if they dress in maintenance uniforms and drive up in a van with utility belts around their waists, they will usually not be questioned by anyone as they move from office to office checking things out.

Without contradictory evidence, how we dress very often signals who we are to the person who is viewing us. That is why dress is such an important piece of corporate cultural pacing. It is important to underscore that overdressing, in many situations, can be just as rapport-breaking as underdressing. Consider calling on mom-and-pop stores in any part of rural America. If you go in looking like a Philadelphia lawyer, you are likely to have barriers erected immediately. While other rapport strategies certainly overcome these problems, why set up obstacles that are likely to cause problems when such obstacles are just as easy to avoid with a little forethought and a little pre-planning regarding what is expected of you?

Most businesses also have protocols that are important to acknowledge. Protocols are often invisible to the outsider, so it is very easy to step out of bounds without even knowing you are yet in the game.

Protocols may center on such procedures as who you speak to first, who gets called by their first name or who gets called Mr. or Ms. They may also affect who lunches with whom, the appropriateness or inappropriateness of smoking in the workplace or having a drink at lunch. Regarding the smoking and drinking questions, we subscribe to the tried-and-true cultural warning: "When in any doubt, don't do it."

Even the acceptance of hospitality gestures often falls into the strange world of varying protocols. For example, how do you handle being offered a cup of coffee when making a call on a client or prospect? Would this change if the client were especially proud of his company's hospitality to outsiders? Would it change if the coffee being offered were the company's own highly regarded special blend? How would you respond to the offer of a taste of your prospect's birthday cake?

Jangled nerves and expanded waistlines notwithstanding, generally the best approach in those situations would be to graciously accept.

Finally, gift giving protocols should be recognized as well. Some organizations have strict rules against accepting business gifts, though most don't. Furthermore, appropriateness in the context of the recipient and business dealings should certainly be considered.

Foreign Culture Pacing

In today's selling world telecommunications, air travel and multinational companies are dissolving international boundaries. Perhaps nowhere is pacing more important than when we're dealing with people whose verbal language, body language, use of time and politics are dissimilar to our own.

How one greets and is greeted in Japan is different than how one greets and is greeted in France. Time protocols relating to business punctuality are completely different in Central America and Northern Europe.

Because I regularly have the opportunity to run international conferences, I've witnessed countless times where failure to culturally pace has either lengthened or destroyed a negotiation.

For example, I recently observed a German salesman attempting to sell a large food contract to the food procurement officer on a large base in Germany. Much of the detail of the contract had already been arranged, and the two men had risen to discuss final details in the hallway. The German salesman moved to within six inches of the procurement officer's face. With each sentence the American took a step backward to regain his comfortable distance. And with each step backwards he took, the German took a step forward. Before long the German salesman had backed the procurement officer to the end of the hall. Speaking to the American later, he reported that they were very close to coming to agreement before he realized that he was not really comfortable with this particular vendor's ability to respond to their needs.

Regional Rapport

Just as foreign cultures differ from our own, so do various cultures within one's own country.

You may have noticed, for example, that very often in the American Deep South a business lunch is much more a social affair than a business affair. In fact, in many parts of the South one is considered rude if he tries to discuss business during a "business lunch." In other parts of the country, a business lunch is exactly for conducting business. And it's the first and lasting topic of conversation throughout the meal. A variation of this is that in many areas people discuss business until the meal arrives and then it becomes a social occasion.

With many business people hopping airplanes and doing business across the country and around the world, and with many business people being transferred from one location to another, some might expect regionally homogenized behavior where everybody is the same or where each corporation has the same expectations as the other corporation. This is simply not the case. We need to use the same pacing skills regarding protocol as we do in the other pacing rapport building skills.

Granted, mass communications and massive transportation abilities are moving cultures toward greater degrees of national, regional and corporate homogeneity. However, it is dangerous to believe that Americans, Germans, Japanese, Southerners or other categories of people are highly similar to most all others in their categories. The exceptions eat up the generalization in short order. Similarly, expectations and protocols differ so greatly from corporation to corporation that it is a better strategy to anticipate differences and watch for them than to expect similarities and not be sensitive to subtle cultural differences.

Another key point to acknowledge and remember is that when people are in the organizations, regions and/or countries, sooner or later the protocols of these organizations, regions, and/or countries get followed in unconscious patterning form. If you run counter to these patterns you'll tend to break rapport on that particular level.

Cultural protocols can be likened to table manners. Transgressing these protocols can elicit a range of responses from smiling amusement to disgusted horror. It's therefore important to pay special attention to the protocols whenever entering a new environment. However, it's not necessary to be overly concerned about stepping out of bounds. Relax in the certainty that if and when you do, if you have sensory acuity you'll sense a reaction. And at that point you can simply backtrack, correct yourself and get back into cultural pacing.

CONTENT PACING

Have you ever had something you desperately wanted to share with someone, but they had something else to talk about first? If you could hardly wait to express what you wanted to say, how closely did you pay attention to what they were telling you? Very often in selling situations we walk into a different agenda than we expected. When this happens the client will often give us cues as to what he needs to get off his chest first, or what he prefers to talk about at that particular moment. In some cases, it's the small talk. In other cases, however, pacing the content that the person wants to talk about can be a very good step towards learning his or her values, predispositions, and priorities.

The *pacing-to-leading continuum* regarding content rapport simply means to meet them where they are, get engrossed in what they are saying and then use a bridging technique to hook something they have said into something that you want to talk about. This happens accidentally all the time. You're talking on a topic and become engrossed, and that reminds you of something else and that carries you to a tangent and that reminds you of something else.

It's a natural patterning, but it's still based on establishing the pacing of the initial content that you and your partner wish to talk about.

Up to this point we've talked about eight levels of pacing: emotional pacing, agreement pacing, posture pacing, tone and tempo pacing, language pacing, values and beliefs pacing, cultural pacing and content pacing. All at once these may seem like a pretty big bite, but feel confident; you are already doing much of this without even knowing it.

Now that you're conscious of many pacing strategies, notice how you are able to implement them within your work-a-day environment. The suggestion here is that to improve any of these skills you do them one at a time. Make it bite-size. Start with the one that interests you the most or that you find the easiest. Many people find posture rapport to be a very good starting point. Emotional rapport is also a favorite.

Continually try meeting people where they are. Notice how they loosen up when you seem to be in their rhythm. Notice how easy it is, once you are in true rhythm with them, to make very subtle changes and bring them into true rhythm with you. Practice. Enjoy. Experiment. In these eight skills alone, there is a wealth of power that's far more than most people ever get in interpersonal influence. Of course, for you they are just a starting point.

SHARED INTEREST

Shared interest can be an extremely strong rapport builder. History has shown us repeatedly that even organizations and cultures that have been in conflict will often join forces and work in harmony when they have a common enemy, or when it is in both of their best interests to defeat a particular problem. For that reason, a high priority should be to demonstrate to the persons within the organization that you are very interested in

them and in helping them achieve goals or overcome obstacles
that are bothering them.

How do you do this? By what you observe around them and
around you, by how you question and by how you respond to
their statements and questions.

Consider this process a form of investigative selling. In
fact, from the very moment that you step into any new organizational environment, your investigative juices should start
pumping. One of the first things you may start noticing is the
formality or informality of the office. Hopefully, your eyes will
go to the wall to see what type of decorations they use. Do they
have productivity charts, or do they have Renoirs? Notice the
reading material around the waiting room. Are there company
publications involved? In that case, speed-read them and start
noticing the opportunities to help.

Do they have productivity problems? Safety problems?
Start cross-referencing with the things you are able to provide,
the solutions you are able to suggest. Do they have *Golf Digest*
on the table? If so, notice whose subscription it is. Most likely it
came to a particular executive. Is that the executive you are
calling on? Is the recipient a decision maker? Make a mental
note of that. In similar fashion notice what is on the walls or on
the desk of a client or prospect you're calling on. Are there civic
awards? Are there diplomas? Achievement awards? What
about motivational slogans?

Does the office reflect a long history, and a sense of strong
ties to the past, or does it appear forward looking, and much
more bent on tomorrow than yesterday?

Classic selling strategies have recommended that, if there are
any indications of what the executive's hobbies are, (perhaps tennis
trophies, or Little League coaching trophies) you should focus on it,
and comment on it, to build rapport. But be cautious here. If you're
simply going through the motions of noticing and praising you can
easily trigger the stereotype of a calculating, insincere salesperson
using an ingratiation tactic. This is about as effective as the public

speaker who tells an obligatory canned joke and then goes on with the dry, dull speech under the assumption that humor in the beginning of the talk will always make an audience more receptive.

If the compliment is done mechanically, most likely you will choose the same item to compliment that every third salesperson that year will have chosen. In that case, you will get the same stereotyped response that one out of every three salespersons that year has gotten.

On the other hand, noting these things and weaving them into your questions and discussions as time goes on will most certainly bring rapport more effectively than such initial hollow flattery as, "Let me compliment you on what a handsome family you have in the picture behind you."

An even more powerful twist on this noticing strategy is to later call attention to the interesting item that's in their office when you are meeting them in a place other than their office. For example, imagine you run into your prospect at a country club and stop to chat a moment about the proposal you are working on. Here is an excellent opportunity to bring up, "You know that Chinese vase that you have in your office? I've thought about that so much in the times since I saw you. It's truly beautiful." Or, "I think you will like what I'm working on because it is highly achievement oriented, and as I recall from the awards on your wall, you can truly appreciate the challenge of working and winning."

AMPLIFYING RAPPORT

Up to this point the types of rapport we have discussed have related mainly to establishing rapport. But what if you already have a fairly strong rapport base built, and you want to amplify the rapport? Are there strategies for doing this? Yes, most certainly there are. When we amplify rapport, in a sense we are moving beyond rapport to an area closer to commitment.

Symbols

A basic strategy for rapport amplification is through the utilization of symbols. As you are already consciously or unconsciously aware, we are symbolic animals. Look around at all the symbols you use, rely on, and appreciate.

Our cars are very often symbols of who we are. They provide much more than transportation. Look on your hands. Are you wearing a class ring? An engagement ring or a wedding ring? These are symbols. How you dress for work symbolizes who you are and how you feel about yourself.

Everywhere we look, symbols tie feelings and experience together into one focal point. For example, surely throughout your lifetime you've been in many situations where you heard an extremely good motivational talk, good sermon or thought-provoking debate. That's probably happened dozens of times. Maybe hundreds. Take a moment right now and jot down twelve of them.

Can you do it? Probably not. Why? Because there's no mental hook. Yet, ask yourself this question: Have you ever gone back to a junk drawer where you have memorabilia, souvenirs, ticket stubs from way back when, and come across something, such as a souvenir you got at your graduation night party, or the small plastic trophy you won at the dance contest in junior high school?

Small symbols like these can appear in our hands, and suddenly we recall the entire evening in vivid detail. In many cases we even re-experience the surge of emotions we felt back then. It's as if these feelings, memories, sounds and images have all been saved and somehow tied or anchored to that simple little symbol.

Could you conjure these emotions and memories up without that symbol? Sure you could. But chances are you wouldn't. Not without something to raise the topic of conversation within your own mind. Not without something to anchor you back to that particular moment in your past.

That's the value of symbols. When a symbol is associated with a memorable, emotion-laden event, this emotional moment seems somehow attached to that symbol as if by an anchor.

Because we intuitively know this and follow it, there are entire industries built around souvenirs at memorable vacation places. On your last vacation, did you pick up any souvenirs? Do you have anything saved to remind you of the good time you had? If so, you know that you are actively involved in this form of symbolic anchoring already. Symbols can be equally powerful in the business contexts also. Let's pretend, for example, that within a business conversation you discover that your client has just received a packet of 5 × 9 pictures of his new granddaughter. His sharing those pictures with you gives you an opportunity to share rapport on how wonderful children are at that age, and how proud he must feel. You would now have a good rapport on that shared appreciation. Can you imagine the impact, several days later, when you send that person a picture frame set and a note saying, "The more I thought about you and your grandchild, the more I became convinced that those pictures needed to be framed and displayed." With such a gesture you've done two very important things. First, you have given a gift that anchors you to a pleasant association. When he looks at that picture frame set, there is a very good probability that the pleasant feelings that he gets related to his grandchild and the pleasant feelings he has about the frame will extend to pleasant feelings about you. The empathy level will be increased.

Reciprocity

The second important amplification strategy relates to reciprocity. In the example above, the picture frame gift most probably created an obligation vacuum. An obligation vacuum simply means that when someone has done something nice for you, then there is a feeling of obligation to fill that void on your side of the reciprocity scale and do something nice for them.

There is a body of scientific knowledge to suggest that on an unconscious as well as conscious level, feelings of reciprocity have a lot to do with how we interact with our environment on a daily basis. You've probably noticed this natural tendency if you've had some friends over to your home for dinner two or three times and they've never reciprocated. If so, there is a very good chance you are starting to feel a little bit irritated with them. You might start thinking of them as freeloaders, people who don't really like you, or people who don't understand the give and take of good relationships.

Let's take this idea one step further and show how it relates to getting behavioral commitment. Assume that you have a client who has been doing business with you for six years. This client has been a very good customer and you already have good rapport. Now here's a very interesting point about the relationship that you have with that client. The odds are that, as happy as that particular customer is with you, regardless of how good your rapport is, *that customer will not recommend you unless one condition is met*. Your customer will not recommend you unless the topic of conversation comes up. Should the topic of conversation come up, and you or your business come to mind, then that person will be delighted to recommend you. However, day in and day out there is little chance the topic of conversation will come up.

How often do you express opinions about how delighted you are with your favorite clothes shop? When is the last time you recommended the person who does your hair? Are you happy with your physician? When is the last time you recommended your physician to someone else?

Chances are you have *never* done these things, no matter how pleased you are with those facets of your life. But if you have, chances are that you recommended your favorite clothing shop because someone complimented you on your outfit. If you mentioned the person who does your hair, it's probably because someone commented on your hair. If you mentioned your physician, it's possibly because someone requested information. Otherwise, you have probably made no such recommendations because the topic of conversation did not come up.

You can bet that your very best clients are in some similar situations. Whether you are selling them computer systems, real estate, insurance, industrial equipment or whatever, chances are you are not getting the recommendations you possibly could get because the topic of conversation does not come up.

Here is how to change that and get the topic of conversation to come up. You can accomplish this by anchoring your rapport to a symbolic gesture and tying it to a symbol the person will use. If your client's name is Bill, you might say to him the next time you meet with him, "Bill, I've been checking my records and I noticed that we've been doing business together for more than six years. You know, I get calls out of the blue from people who are in businesses similar to yours, and they ask me to come in and present what I have. Quite often, neither my secretary nor I ever think to ask how they happened to call me. Bill, I have to believe that often they are calling because my good customers like you have mentioned me in the course of conversation." Then you take out some symbol that will be meaningful to Bill. It can be a semi-expensive high-quality writing instrument, a leather portfolio, or any gift that specifically relates to Bill's needs or predispositions. At that point you say, "Bill, what I want to do is thank you for all the times you've recommended me to your friends. And I'd like to give you this small token of my appreciation for all the help you've been to me in the past, and for all the recommendations I've not stopped to thank you for till now, Bill." Shake his hand, hand him the gift and say, "Thanks, buddy. Thanks for your recommendations."

Bill is probably too nice a person to look you in the eye and say, "My friend, I've never recommended you in my ever-loving life." And Bill probably won't hand you back the gift and say, "I really don't deserve it." No, Bill will most likely smile and say, "I've been very pleased with the way you've handled our business up to this point, and I'm sure in the future I will continue to be pleased. I'll be happy to recommend you every chance I get."

The symbol is there to remind him. Will he do it time and time again? It depends on whether the symbol reminds him in the proper context. If you already have rapport, Bill is already pleased with what you are able to do. Bill would, under any other circumstances, if the topic of conversation came up, be willing to make the recommendation. The symbol can, therefore, conjure up those good feelings and inclinations to recommend you when opportunities arise.

There are four ways to make symbols particularly valuable or meaningful to the recipient. The first, and most obvious way, is to make them expensive. But expensiveness is not a requirement for value. In fact, very often it's not a good idea to give an expensive gift. Under no circumstances would we want to break a values rapport agreement that one does not buy business from another. Goodwill is commonly acceptable, bribes are not.

Since the IRS limits business gift deductions to $25 or less, there is little chance that anyone you do business with would consider any item in that range a bribe. However, a $380 color television set might be in questionable taste, and many governmental and corporate offices take a very dim view of executives receiving gifts.

A second way to make something valuable or meaningful is to make it unique or scarce. This can relate to novelty value—something that the person has never seen before. A special seasoning for your client who is a gourmet cook would be unique and probably in good taste.

A third way to make a gift meaningful is to make it symbolic of something greater. The diploma on your wall is probably in that category. The paper and frame itself have little value, but it all represents hard work and achievement. Award certificates and certificates of recognition fall in this category.

The photograph taken of the foursome in the pro-am golf tournament falls in this category, as would a meaningful picture of a good time you had with the client.

A fourth way to add value is to make your gift personalized. Can you recall getting a very nice typeset name badge at a trade show, conference, or convention? Because your name was so beautifully typeset, you may have found it difficult to throw that badge away. But what could be less useful than a used trade show or convention name badge? The attribute of being personalized with your very own beautiful name gave it more value. Now if that level of value works on a name badge, imagine how it can enhance a well-chosen executive gift. Therefore, the symbol would enhance the relationship more because the personalization would enhance the symbol.

Returning to the thanks for recommending approach, now that we understand varying forms of enhancing a gift's meaningfulness or value, you may say, "Well, if they give me a recommendation then they are doing nothing more than paying off a debt." There is some merit to this. Yet it's also possible that if the feelings toward you were genuine, and if you've paced them well, that it will not be the payment of a debt so much as the expression of a legitimate feeling.

The irony of this is that if the latter is true, the person recommending you will feel more strongly about you after he continually recommends you than he would have had it never come up. In similar fashion, another way of increasing and amplifying rapport is to get your satisfied customers to write you a letter of recommendation. In terms of attitude formation, the written word is very powerful. The most powerful form of this amplification mode is to get your client to write a letter recommending you in his or her own words. Even though the writing may be an inconvenience, if the client does it he or she will psychologically justify that effort by rationalizing that you indeed were worth it.

Of course, your client may decline and say, "I'm really happy with you, but our schedules are so busy I just can't take the time." At that point, you can take a drop-back position and say, "Would it be all right for me to draft something, and if it meets with your approval, you would just give it to your secretary for your signature?" This will have value too, not just as a letter of recommendation to show to future prospects but also as an enhancer of your value to that person.

If you want to establish double value after they have complied and given you that special favor, then you in turn give them a symbolic gift to anchor that recommendation to the gift.

The context of this is important. The implication should *not* be, "If you will write me a letter of recommendation, I will give you the gift." There are several reasons for that. The most obvious is that it makes it appear that their good word can be bought with a gift. The second reason is if they do write it to earn a gift they will be less psychologically moved in the direction of rapport amplification than if they did it for little or no forthcoming reward. Then you can amplify further by giving them an unexpected symbol as a token of your appreciation for this tremendous relationship and mutual admiration that you have.

By the way, if they do write a letter of recommendation for *any* reason it will generally have some psychological effect on them in terms of leaning more toward a preference for you. The movement may be slight but there will still be movement. That's why, over the years, there have been so many contests based on telling why you like a product in 25 words or less. People trying to win a contest by writing why they like a product will psychologically move toward liking that product more. Of course, not everybody will be moved in the same way or to the same extent. But, overall, the patterning that we use psychologically will predict positive movement in the direction of what we write down.

Up to this point, we have been talking about anchoring positive feelings with tangible symbols such as gifts. It is important to recognize that both positive *and* negative associations can be attached to gifts or to anything that we see, hear, feel, smell or taste. For example, do you sometimes feel a little queasy in a doctor's office or hospital at the smell of that antiseptic atmosphere? Are there certain songs or sounds that bring forth emotional responses of happiness, sadness or longing in you? Have you ever found an old souvenir and re-experienced the memories and fun you had on that trip when you happened to pick it up?

Positive and negative feelings can be anchored to anything that we take in through our senses, not just tangible gifts. For this reason, we should be careful to avoid anchoring unpleasant associations to us, to what we give, to our voices, or to anything relating to our business or products.

Have you ever noticed on television that the rosier the news from the government the higher the official who announces it? Whereas, terrible or poor economic news is usually announced by someone lower within the bureaucracy. The reason for this is simple. Those in power want positive news associated with them. They don't want negative news associated with them, even though it comes from the same department. So rather than have their face, image, or voice associated with negative feelings, they will have an underling do it.

It's also important to avoid anchoring strong negative associations to gifts, such as apology gifts. If the symbolic gesture of giving something by way of apology is necessary to soothe the moment, we recommend a *consumable gift*. A free drink as an apology for an airline delay, or a box of candy or fresh flowers as an apology for an inconvenience to an office manager would be examples of good consumable gifts. The point is that while gift giving is a goodwill stimulator in many contexts, you don't want a long-lasting gift to remind your client of a past screw-up again and again over time.

An apparent reversal of this recommendation is on quiz or game shows where the contestants win consolation prizes. Consolation prizes are given for two major reasons. One is to gain promotional dollars from those who give the consolation prizes, and the second is to help the audience psychologically dismiss the person who has lost. The consolation prizes are really not of great benefit in many cases to the contestants who are getting consoled. Put yourself in their place. In one moment you are striving to win $50,000, and suddenly another contestant comes forth and wins, or you choose the wrong number, or something happens where you lose everything; as a consolation prize they give you a year's supply of dog biscuits and a twelve-speed blender. The dog biscuits and the blender both are going to be offered to you whether you have a dog or the need for a blender. That's the nature of the promotion.

Over this next year, do you suppose that every time you used that blender you'd smile and say, "Well, at least I got a $39 blender out of it." Or each time you used that blender might you think of yourself as someone who came very close to winning but lost on national television?

When we want repeat business we need to be careful to avoid anchoring unpleasant associations. Carried further, if you must share unpleasant news, it's better to share it in their environment, not yours.

Consider the cultures within the organization and business environment you're operating in, and be especially certain your strategies involve appropriate protocol and appropriate behavior. While these compliance strategies will work in most situations, if they are considered in bad taste they can backfire and break rapport at a values level. Testing the waters with such questions as, "May I ask you a special favor?" or "Could you help me with something?" go a long way by softening the blow if your request is indeed out of the appropriate realm of protocol for the organization.

QUESTIONS AND ANSWERS ABOUT RAPPORT

Question: *I'm still unsure what you mean about rapport. Isn't it just being liked?*

Answer: Being liked is often a by product of rapport. And since liking is often based on similarity of styles, values, and communication patterns, we might think of it as often accompanying rapport. Think of rapport as the attraction of another person's attention and trust that you understand them and their reality to such an extent that you can support, help or enhance them in the context of your relationship.

If that's too wordy, simply think of rapport as how responsive a person is to you and your positive intentions. How do you get that? By first being responsive to them through pacing their patterns.

Question: *Who do you try to gain rapport with? Everybody?*

Answer: You try to gain rapport with those people that you need to influence—especially family and friends. But in business situations, concentrate mainly on your clients, prospects *and* those people who influence them. These people may include the co-workers, the secretaries, the receptionist, and even bosses. Unfortunately, it's not always clear whether or not you are talking to the full decision-maker in many cold-call situations. In fact, some estimates are that over 60 percent of all sales calls are made on the wrong person, the wrong decision-maker or someone who has incomplete decision-making abilities. Because of this, it's often good to qualify the prospect up front by asking the person, "Ms. Johnson, as you and I discuss these plans and come to agreement on the best course of action, is there anyone else that we may need to include in this decision-making process in order for us to move ahead?" The answer to that question will often give you information regarding obvious people who formally need to give approval. You most certainly need to influence them, and (unless you're in telemarketing) you probably are going to want to get face-to-face with them in order to influence them properly.

Even if they do not indicate a number of other people involved in the decision-making process, don't jump to the conclusion that there is not a multitude of influencers out there. In fact, from the moment you enter any office, you need to start looking at everyone as if she or he may be the pivotal vote you need to get your proposition accepted.

Start with the receptionist. Not only are receptionists fountains of knowledge about what is going on in the office, they also are often the initial gatekeepers to the organization. They can keep you out, or help you get in. If this is true with the receptionists, it's even more true with executive secretaries. Even though executive secretaries probably make much less money than you, they often have the power to undermine or enhance your business relationships on their turfs. Here you have true gatekeepers.

In many cases an executive secretary also has a strong vote in purchase decisions. Usually this vote is more informal than formal. Because personal secretaries are such an integral part of how executives make decisions, they often may be a deciding factor on who gets business.

Question: *Are there occasions when you need to break rapport?*

Answer: Sure. You do it all the time. For example, on an airplane, if you don't want to engage in conversation with the talkative person next to you, you probably break rapport by reading, looking disinterested, and generally having a different agenda than what they wish to talk about.

If you wish to become less involved with an unpleasant person or someone you're angry with, notice that you don't make eye contact with them, that you don't follow their body language patterns, and that you tend to put up an invisible wall between you and them.

Often we break rapport unconsciously, and thus we don't even notice certain people in our environment. Waiters and waitresses occasionally fall in this category. Most any waiter or waitress can tell about the amazing conversations they are privy to because people have psychologically dismissed them as non-persons and have continued very private exchanges in spite of their being present. As you get better in your rapport skills you realize the key to being very good versus being average is that you will not break rapport unintentionally.

Question: *Isn't all of this somewhat manipulative?*

Answer: Yes. It certainly can be. Once again, let's differentiate between influence and manipulation. It is more than a semantic difference. If your outcome and your client's outcome are tied together, and you're facilitating the client's achieving his or her outcome through your strategy, then it could be considered either positive manipulation, or win-win influence.

On the other hand, if your outcome and your client's outcome are at odds with one another, if you are trying to sell something you know he or she cannot use, or if you are trying to persuade him or her for something that would not be in his or her best interest, then it is indeed negative manipulation.

Whether we wish to accept it or not, we cannot *not* communicate. Furthermore, whenever we communicate with other humans we are to some degree affecting their behaviors and their attitudes. If you set up an incentive contest within your organization, are you manipulating? Influencing? Sure you are, but it's positive.

These insights, techniques and strategies we're sharing can be used for good productive reasons, or for not-so-good reasons. They can be constructive or destructive, just like a hammer or any other tool that can be used to build or destroy. The deciding variable is the integrity of the person using them.

Question: *Does this mean that I will sell everyone?*

Answer: No, not at all. Some people you call on won't need what you have to offer. Other people will need it but will not qualify for it. What these skills can do continually is keep you from not selling. They can keep you from undermining your own best efforts by making mistakes that are very common to most salespeople and managers.

As you learn, practice, apply, and relearn the lessons here, you'll find your percentage of closing sales will increase dramatically. Not only that, but your enjoyment of selling will increase dramatically too.

Question: *How much rapport do you need to get the job done?*

Answer: That depends on your job and your obstacles. Small influence moves require less rapport than large moves, just as small buildings require less foundation than huge sky-scrapers. Be generous with your rapport efforts. Establishing rapport is like creating fertile soil for future bountiful harvests.

The time to build alliances is before you need them, not after you need them. So, in that context, whether your client is large or small, treat that client as if he or she represents a thousand good referrals. Within the organization that you are calling upon, whether the person is powerful or not powerful, treat that person as if someday he or she may be the key gatekeeper or decision-maker on a project that means a lot to you.

Question: *What if they don't respond to my rapport strategies?*

Answer: If the rapport strategies are done right, they will respond. What is needed is flexibility. If one approach isn't working, try something else. Often what seems like resistance is just the inability to immediately get into their reality—the patterns they're operating with. For example, awhile back, my six year old daughter was having a great deal of difficulty getting to sleep one night. I decided to use some of these pacing-and-leading strategies to help her get to sleep. Our outcomes were matched. She was tired but over-stimulated and did want to get to sleep. I was also tired, and I wanted her to get to sleep. I sat on the side of her bed and we talked in the same tone and tempo. Then she put her head down and I started talking to her in a rather rhythmic pattern that matched her breathing. Slowly I became more calm, more rhythmic, and more relaxing in the way I talked to her.

After about five minutes, she seemed to be breathing smoothly in quiet rapport. I gave her a suggestion that in just a moment I was going to give her a very special kiss that was going to make her feel oh-so relaxed and oh-so sleepy that she was going to drift right into dreamland. I then leaned forward and gave her a very gentle kiss and whispered, "Goodnight, Sunshine. I love you."

As I eased myself from the side of the bed, in a wide-awake voice, she said, "Daddy, I'm still not sleepy."

Reflexively, without missing a beat (in her alert tone and tempo) I exclaimed, "Of course you're not sleepy." And then referring to the stuffed doll that she was holding, "Because Amber's not asleep yet. Do you suppose you could help Amber get to sleep?"

She said yes, she thought she could.

"Well, how would you hold Amber to help her go to sleep?" I asked.

"Like this," she answered as she nestled closer to her doll.

"Is Amber very comfortable?" I asked.

"Very comfortable, Daddy," she said.

"Now, I want you to hold Amber and I want you to help Amber fall sound asleep. Do you think you could be that good to help her to fall asleep?"

"Oh yes, I think so."

"Good. I'll come back and check on you in five minutes to see if you have helped Amber to get to sleep all right." With that I left the room.

When I returned to the room five minutes later both my daughter and her doll, Amber, were sound asleep. For some reason the calm, soothing words that night, pacing her breathing and getting her more and more relaxed weren't working. So as soon as I got that signal I immediately switched rapport strategies and got into her reality on a content level—something she was interested in at that very moment. In doing so I helped the two of us achieve our mutual outcome of her falling, comfortably and securely asleep.

Question: *Can one rapport mismatch undermine me?*

Answer: It's possible, but not probable. Whenever destructive mismatches occur they usually happen in the cultural or values and beliefs areas. For example, you may call on a person who has an idiosyncrasy about your size, your ethnic background, your mannerisms or looks. (Perhaps you look like the ex-spouse that person feels very hostile towards.) In such cases the person will likely have difficulty establishing rapport with you immediately. If you sense that mismatch and if you respond appropriately you will be able to overcome this obstacle. In many cases, by overcoming an obstacle you'll establish an even stronger rapport than you would have had there been no obstacle to overcome.

Have you ever had the experience of meeting someone that you initially didn't care for, but as you got to know them a little bit more—their values, their inclinations, their interests—you found yourself liking them more and more to where you became great friends over time? It's a similar situation. Overcoming an initial emotional obstacle can be like cresting a hill and enjoying the momentum of coasting in comparison to the climb up.

Question: *Are there major rapport obstacles I need to watch out for?*

Answer: Yes. Their idiosyncrasies and yours. Theirs you will note by watching, listening, questioning and pacing. Yours may be a little more difficult because they are a part of your reality. Beware of judging and labeling in the course of your interactions with a client; this means mentally as well as verbally. Rest assured if you are sitting in front of a client thinking, "Boy, this SOB is difficult to get along with," that emotion will probably show through in the form of your very slight non-verbal cues. Your eye contact will be less. You will make slight grimaces with your lips. You'll possibly give off sighs of frustration, and you'll undermine your ability to do business effectively.

Labels are good for explaining and educating, for pointing out differences and calling attention to nuances, but they are not very good for interacting. When we label people we tend to respond to the label and not to the individual person. We start reacting to them as if they are a stereotype, and we begin missing their individual needs and predispositions.

While rapport does not require liking, liking is a very nice thing to have when trying to establish rapport, or establish any business relationship. Some people in my seminars have raised the question, "How do you get clients to like you?" The rapport strategies that I have outlined will help to some degree, but a psychological underpinning is simply, "*Like them first!*" If you feel positively towards them, all the nonverbal cues that you give unconsciously will come forth in that manner of liking. It will help them release their own defensiveness. It will keep them from having to put up guards to protect themselves.

Comedian McLean Stevenson quipped, "My wife tricked me into marrying her... She said she liked me." You may find it interesting that Joe Girard, noted for being the most successful car salesman in the world, every single month of the year sent a holiday greeting card to every one of his car customers. While the cards, pictures and greetings varied from month to month, every single month on the inside the card said the same thing: "I like you." As Joe explained to social psychologist Robert Cialdini, "There's nothing else on the card. Nothin' but my name. I'm just telling 'em I like 'em." If the best in the world uses this liking strategy, it bears attention from the rest of us.

By the way, we highly recommend Cialdini's book, *Influence*, Wm. Morrow & Company, 1984.

Question: *Once I have rapport, can I lose it?*

Answer: Definitely so. Think of rapport as a balance scale. As you build rapport, you're adding balance to the positive side. If suddenly you drop a highly valued negative weight on the other side, you can either neutralize the positive balance you've built or you can outweigh all the positive effects. Normally, this type of bombshell would be in the area of values rapport. For example, if someone makes you question his or her integrity or their ability to perform in the way that they are representing themselves, then you are going to suddenly question whether you should advance. In similar fashion, if you are making a presentation and you mention something that makes them suddenly break rapport with you, you backtrack, find where the trouble spot is, handle it appropriately (as you will learn in later sections of this program), and then pace, pace, pace. Stated more simply, if you lose rapport you need to backtrack and recapture momentum where you had strong rapport working for you. Should that rapport break have been from a values issue, you re-establish a values caricature, proceed with the pacing skills we've already established, and then utilize the additional influence skills that are yet to come.

In some cases, even an interruption can be a break in rapport because it moves the person from the mindset that you have established and puts him or her onto a different track. Thus when interrupted you back up and get him or her re-established on the right track with the right momentum through a brief recap of what you have mutually covered to that point, paying close attention to pacing them on as many levels as you can.

Question: *Once I've paced them to the point of establishing rapport am I ready to lead them?*

Answer: Not necessarily. Just because they are willing to let you scratch them doesn't mean that you yet know where they itch. You need to systematically identify their needs and success criteria. These steps take the questioning skills found in the next segment.

CHAPTER THREE

Identifying Needs
and
Establishing Criteria

IDENTIFYING NEEDS

In your current selling situation you probably have a series
of qualifying questions to ascertain whether you are speaking
to the right buyer and what the buyer's purchase needs might
be. These questions usually center around who, what, where,
when, why and how questions. For example, if your area were
real estate home sales you would qualify your walk-in prospect
with questions relating to:

1. Who will be living in the home?
2. What size home are they thinking about?
3. What particular area do they prefer?
4. What particular style of home and special features do
   they have in mind?
5. How soon are they hoping to move?
6. Where do they live now?
7. Do they now rent or own?
8. What have they looked at so far?
9. How familiar are they with the area?
10. How familiar are they with financing?
11. What price home are they thinking of?
12. Who is involved in the purchase decision?

If you were selling premium and incentive programs to
corporations, your standard fact-finding questions would be
oriented toward:

1. What goods and services does the organization sell?
2. What kind of sales force? How large? Commissioned?
3. How large is the distribution area? How many customers and potential customers are there?
4. Who are the client's major customers?
5. Are there ongoing safety, productivity or quality control incentive programs in effect?
6. What are major problems and opportunities? Image?
   Safety? Sales? Seasonal fluctuation? Productivity?
7. What promotions have worked and not worked in the
   past?

8. What materials are available telling about the company, its products and its services?

9. Who are the major competitors and how do they compare in size, sales and promotion?

10. Is there an ad agency involved, and if so, how?

11. What size budget is allocated?

12. Who is involved in making promotion decisions? Who decides? Who can veto? What's their time frame?

Virtually every industry has its standard list of imperative who, what, where, when, why and how questions for qualifying what the prospect or client should buy. Yet what about identifying the prospect's or client's personal buying patterns?

In this chapter we will introduce the incredible power our habitual patterns exert on us and our organizations. Then we'll specifically identify, explain and teach you to utilize the major patterns people use in buying situations.

PATTERNS

Our minds have extremely sophisticated wiring, but relatively simple functions. Since psychological research by Harvard professor George A. Miller in the 1950s, it has been commonly recognized that in most cases we can consciously attend to a maximum of five to nine variables at any given time. If we go beyond that we have to break them into chunks that we will remember separately. For example, phone numbers, which are typically seven digits, are divided for easier remembering into three digits and then a pattern of four. By adding an area code in front of that you get beyond the nine, so it becomes all the more important to chunk apart a small piece of information, the area code, from the rest of the number. In other words, patterns within patterns are formed to help us remember longer patterns.

When you first learned the alphabet, you probably didn't learn the letters straightforwardly. You probably learned it through the little ABC song. Even as an adult you may find yourself going through a rhythmic pattern if alphabetical order doesn't pop into your head immediately. For example, what letter comes after "T?" Some people have to go back through the entire song beginning with "A," whereas others have a smaller chunk and start with "Q, R, S, T." Since we are attending to only five to nine pieces of information at any given time, we have to take a lot of mental shortcuts.

When you enter a room, you typically don't consider whether or not the floor will support you. Your mind, hopefully, doesn't wander into such questions as whether there is a tiger in the next room ready to leap out and grab you. Will a meteor hit or will that chair really support you? In that manner, we have formed stereotypes. This floor looks like all other floors that I've seen, so without even thinking I will go ahead and step on it. Stereotypes, therefore, are patterns or large chunks of information distilled into one, easy-to-grasp, predigested, mental bite. Just as patterns are very important to us, completing patterns is very important to us. If someone were to play an incomplete piano scale, *do re me fa sol la ti*, we would feel this urge to hit, sing, or respond to the last note, *do*. When we observe that we are creatures of habit, we are implying we are creatures of patterns, for habits are also a form of patterning. All of nature seems to work in patterns. And because we are indeed part of nature we too work in patterns. In fact, virtually everything we do individually and organizationally is in patterns.

An example of organizational chunking patterns is described by Peters and Waterman in *In Search of Excellence*. "The small group is the most visible of chunking devices. Small groups are, quite simply, the basic organizational building blocks of excellent companies." (p.126) They go on to explain that while managers usually consider departments, divisions or strategic units as the basic organizational building blocks, it's the smaller-chunked task forces, teams, project centers, skunk works and quality circles that are the action-oriented achievement centers. It's here that large problems are chunked down to manageable size and acted upon by people who grasp the situation.

Another way of chunking for business excellence is explained in the communication strategy package *3-Sigma* by Reese, Reese, Spechler and Spechler. Strategies for communication excellence within organizations are developed by systematic modeling procedures based on the behaviors of the top performers in the company or field. (Technically those are at or above the third standard deviation on a bell-shaped curve, thus the name 3-Sigma.)

More specifically, by using a small segment of the bell-shaped curve the chunk size of the general business population is reduced in two ways. First, there's a smaller chunk of the population, and second, that small chunk carries the highest level of performance. The next step is to find the strategies and patterns that the people in this select group use in common. These strategies and patterns are then chunked into specific learning units that can be taught and monitored within the rest of the organization.

Some psychologists suggest that more than 95 percent of our behaviors are in small-pattern chunks. Have you ever lost your keys? If so, there is a high likelihood that you have a pattern of places to look for them. My pattern is to look first on my dresser, because that's where they are supposed to be. If they're not there then I immediately go to the pants that I wore the evening before and check those pockets. If they're not in those pockets, I check a particular table where my keys occasionally turn up. The next step is normally the kitchen, and then my favorite chair where they could have fallen. Now here is the interesting part. If those keys show up in none of those places, then I virtually always find myself back looking on the dresser again, the place that I already looked and already saw that my keys were not there. Next, I recheck my pants pockets.

After that, the familiar table, the kitchen, and my favorite chair, asking all the time in typical pattern, "Has anybody seen my keys?" It takes about two or three times through these patterns to become convinced that my keys are not in any of these particular areas. I still may look in those same places, even a fourth time, because my keys have been there so many times it is part of my pattern.

Everywhere we look we see patterns. Patterns are so important to us that they form our reality. Perhaps you have gone through a formal receiving line where the protocol and patterning is so rigid that if you say anything other than the obligatory "Hello" "How are you?" " I'm doing fine" you probably won't even be heard. The information won't sink in. Since you understand that, it should come as no surprise to you that we also make decisions based on certain predictable patterns. In other words, we tend to make decisions in the same way we have made similar decisions before.

All this pattern talk lays the foundation for this important premise: people buy within their own predictable patterns. These patterns are principally based on how they mentally sort information. Therefore, when you are able to recognize these mental sorting patterns you are in a position to understand the required steps they go through to arrive at decisions. If what you offer aligns with how they decide, then you have rapport and you are on your way toward satisfying their pattern needs as well as their outcome needs.

You've heard the rhetorical question, "Is the glass half empty or is the glass half full?" In that context you've seen that how a person perceives the proverbial glass affects how he experiences and responds to the value of the glass. Thus, mental sorting simply means how a person habitually organizes and patterns information. In the glass example some people habitually sort for what is missing (they're in the half-empty group) and some habitually sort for what is present (they're the half-full group).

There are many ways to sort information. What follows are the key sorting patterns that generally affect buying decisions:

THE AUTHORITY SORT

Pretend that you are going to go out to spend a lot of money on a new stereo. How do you decide which stereo is going to be best for you? Think about this for a moment.

Initially there are only three probable starting points: (1) your own personal inclinations, (2) other people's inclinations, or (3) other sources such as the mass media, consumer reports, advertising and the like.

If your inclination is toward yourself it probably relates to how the equipment sounds to you, how it looks to you, how you intuit or feel about it. Or you may approach the decision from a logic standpoint, using any available data you can find.

The second starting point would be to consult someone else who knows a lot about stereo equipment and ask his or her opinion; or to see what others have in their own homes; or to discuss purchase ideas with others for their reactions about what you should get in a stereo. The third initial strategy would relate to looking at such sources as technical data, consumer reports, stereo critics, or articles about what is trendy. This application would usually relate back to a logic-based analysis.

Your clients and prospects also go through these sorting options. Their authority sort, like yours, will center on (1) their own internal evaluation system, (2) how other persons respond to the proposition at hand, or (3) what has been written or documented regarding the choices.

One of our clients was selling a seminar to a large corporation. He found that the area manager basically had an authority sort that relied on external data and thus needed to have magazine articles and trade publications presented to him before he could comfortably decide on accepting the seminar. After the decision was made, the division manager's approval was the next hurdle in the sale. The division manager had virtually no interest in what magazines said about the seminar. Instead, she asked that a segment of the seminar be presented to her to see if it influenced her in the way the seminar presenter said it would.

Implicit in this example are two of the three authority sorts you're likely to encounter – data authority and self authority. Since our client was familiar with sorting processes he found the adjustment between these two styles easy to make, and did not fall into the what-the-hell-do-they-want-from-me syndrome when the presentation demands changed.

THE MISMATCH/MATCH SORT

Mismatchers fall into two general categories: Counter Example Sorters and Polarity Sorters.

Counter Example Sorters

Counter Example Sorters are the people who find it necessary to generate alternatives to what you're presenting. Therefore, if you present an idea requiring agreement, they'll typically present you with a list of "yes-buts" that will show you why your idea won't work. If, on the other hand, you present how something won't work they will give you a list of reasons why it will. For example, you may have been in a meeting where a new marketing strategy was being hammered out and had someone from accounting who begins to list all of the reasons why the campaign cannot possibly work. Or you may have experienced saying to a prospect or client who is a counter-example sorter, "I have some serious reservations about whether we can get this project out on time," only to have her provide a list of reasons why it could be accomplished.

It's important to recognize that what we're talking about here is a *habitual* pattern that triggers automatically. This person is different from the individual who occasionally lists objections.

One of our more entrepreneurial clients maintains a position on his staff of someone who is a counter-example sorter whom he calls his "no-man." Whenever he has a new idea or venture he carefully presents it to his "no-man" as an idea that will definitely work. His no-man, of course, immediately generates a list of reasons why it won't work, thus identifying many possible pitfalls in the project that our client might have otherwise missed in his enthusiasm. Just as our client utilizes no-man, when you recognize a counter example sorter (whether a client, prospect or co-worker) you can lead that person with either a positive or negative statement that will cause him to generate either a negative or positive list of counter examples.

Polarity Sorters

Polarity sorters respond automatically with the opposite response you're trying to generate. If you say, "Let's go" they say, "Let's stay." If you say, "Let's decide later," they say, "No, let's decide now."

Remember the Uncle Remus story where Brer Rabbit begs to Brer Fox, "You can do anything, but please don't throw me in the briar patch?" Well, he was banking on Brer Fox offering a polarity response and doing the opposite—throwing him in the briar patch where he would be safe.

Thus the key for dealing effectively with polarity responders is to suggest the opposite. For example, one of our clients in the specialty advertising industry recognized one of his clients as a polarity responder and decided to play to his processing pattern. On the next call he prefaced his promotional presentation with, "Here is a program that you won't be able to afford, but I want to show it to you anyway." The polarity responder immediately took it upon himself to prove he could afford the program by buying it. Besides enjoying the profitability of the sale, our client reported that by letting the polarity responder function naturally, the sale was made with virtually none of the tension and wrangling that had been present in their earlier encounters.

By the way, our client still needed to give his client good value program or repeat business would not have been forthcoming.

Matching Sorters

Perhaps you've had the opportunity of bringing an innovative new product into the market, and been faced with the situation of having many of your clients say to you, "But isn't that *just like*...?" In such cases you understand how matching sorters operate—they first process for similarities.

All of us have heard the man who makes the statement that all women are alike or the woman who sees all men as alike. Through their matching sorts they observe the similarities but miss the varying attributes of the individuals of the opposite gender. While it might seem that they are missing something, matchers are generally quite comfortable with their tendencies to perceive similarities more than differences. So when persuading them the key is to play to their comfort zones by stressing the similarities between what you are proposing and what they are familiar with.

For example, recently we were making a proposal to a matching sorter (a corporate V.P. of marketing) to sell his company seminars based on the materials you're learning in this book. We gained rapport, identified his needs, established his success criteria in terms of his personal and organizational objectives, and, maintaining rapport, offered our plan stressing similarities with what he had seen and used in the past. We acknowledged major differences in how our program differed from others, but didn't stress them.

As he listened to our presentation points he continually translated the seminar points into general categories of what he's used before. While we saw major differences, he saw sameness. And since he was buying, his comfort zone held priority over ours in terms of categorizing.

After answering a number of his concerns we summarized our points of agreement and requested action. He said he liked our approach and was certain he would get approval and funding for us.

As we were beginning to leave he gave us a broad smile and said, "I've really got to compliment you on how you've packaged your ideas. You know, I've been in this business for twenty years, and I can tell you there's really nothing new under the sun."

We smiled, agreed and left with his cooperation commitment.

More people use a matching sort than a mismatching sort. That's one reason standardized franchises are doing so well across the country. The late Ray Kroc, guru of standardization, recognized the masses' desire for feeling confident that the food they got at one McDonald's would have the same taste and quality as the food in any other McDonald's. What he provided was consistency of quality, service, cleanliness and menu to a population sorting for sameness in a world of change.

By noticing people's habitual patterns of matching or mismatching, your persuasive abilities will be enhanced through recognition of how to frame your proposals to meet their models of the world.

THE GENERAL/SPECIFIC SORT

Perhaps nowhere in communication is there more misunderstanding than when we find two people who are talking about different-sized chunks of information. The general-sorting person needs to have the overall picture in order to be receptive to an idea, whereas the specific-sorting person needs to have details and more details and *more* details in order to be receptive to an idea.

If you happen to be a general sorter you can probably recall times you were bored into high levels of frustration by someone who felt compelled to feed you detail after detail about information you already knew more about than you cared to.

If you're a specific sorter you can probably recall your frustration in dealing with someone who was only willing to give you the big picture, leaving out all the important details one needs to make a well-considered decision.

General sorters start assembling their child's bicycle with hardly a glance at the instructions. Specific sorters not only read the instructions carefully, but double check and count the pieces, comparing them to how the instructions describe them.

Specific sorters are likely to believe that if you keep your eye on the pennies the dollars will take care of themselves. General sorters are more likely to believe that if you keep your eye on the dollars the pennies will take care of themselves.

Over the years we have dabbled in the real estate market, buying and renovating apartment buildings, raising the caliber of tenants and rents and selling after a few years of depreciation—an interesting and profitable hobby.

Several times we've negotiated successfully with specific sorters who had driven a number of potential buyers away with a flood of what seemed to the buyers to be nit-picky, unreasonable details and procedures, such as how to deal with back rents that may or may not be collected in the future, who pays for termite inspections, who pays for negotiable closing costs, a quarter percent more on the purchase money mortgage, the nature of late payment penalties, promising to give the tenant in #5 a new refrigerator, how many days to spend "thinking about" each new change in the contract, and availability or lack of availability of the negotiating principals.

Usually the sum total of the actual out-of-pocket costs of conceding a plethora of minor detail points was less than a couple thousand dollars – an amount we were glad to pay for buying tens of thousands below what we had already ascertained the real estate was worth to us.

The danger of approaching a general sorter with a specific-sorter strategy is in boring or frustrating the general sorter into dropping out of the game. The danger of approaching a specific sorter with a general-sorter strategy is in building frustration and distrust through not supplying or satisfying enough details for the specific sorter to feel comfortable before proceeding.

These, however, are not totally static states of being. It's possible to operate with both general and specific sorting patterns, but for most it takes discipline to stretch into one's less favorite mode. However, our negotiating, sales and training experience has demonstrated repeatedly that this stretch is well worth the effort.

THE PAST ASSURANCE/FUTURE POSSIBILITIES SORT

Think about investing in a mutual fund. Would you be more inclined to go with one that has a demonstrated good track record, or would you be more inclined to put your money in a more speculative, high risk, high return fund?

People who sort for past assurances respond to offers that provide them with a history of evidence. They *rest assured* that their choice is already proven over time.

People who sort for future possibilities are more blue sky oriented. They enjoy the possibilities that lie within open-ended opportunities. They're attracted to bigger risks for greater potential payoffs.

In training salespeople working in the time-share condominium industry, we've found their understanding of this sorting pattern to be very important. For example, salespeople do best with past assurance sorters when they ask, "How much money have you spent over the past ten years on your vacations?" They generally come with a figure between $10,000 and

$15,000. From that basis they quickly show the person how a mere $5,000 investment will pay for itself in less than half that time.

In contrast, when talking to future possibilities sorters the salesperson will raise questions about future skyrocketing inflation over the next 20 years and what that will do to rates at vacation resorts. Before the salesperson completes the presentation the future costs total from $30,000 to $40,000 compared to the mere $5,000 investment that can be taken care of now. Suggestions of future real estate appreciation add the icing to the cake for these blue-sky oriented future possibilities sorters.

When closing a sale with a person who falls at either one of these extremes be sure to match his or her sorting style, or what you're proposing will often break rapport by moving them toward advantages that feel to them like threatening disadvantages.

PROBLEM AVOIDANCE/GOAL ORIENTATION SORT

Similar to the Past Assurances/Future Possibilities Sort is the Problem Avoidance/Goal Orientation Sort. This sorting pattern recognizes that some people are more highly motivated to move *away from* problems and others are more highly motivated to move *toward* positive outcomes.

If your customer is problem-avoidance oriented, you will not be effective trying to sell him on achieving goals without first showing how the problems will be taken care of. If a customer is highly goal-oriented, a problem-avoidance approach will seem too tentative and negative to enthuse.

Understanding your client's convincer strategies is essential to effective harnessing of your client's objectives.

Sometimes selling situations come down to win/lose propositions. A company may use only one or two suppliers of what you sell, so for you to get its business they will have to drop one of their suppliers, or they will have to go to some extra trouble to include you. If you find yourself meeting resistance on this level, you may find the problem-avoidance goal-orientation sort to be extremely valuable. In this situation you'd want to know whether the person you're talking with is more problem-avoidance oriented or more goal-oriented. You would most likely ask, "When you last added a new supplier, what was your motivation?" If they say something like, "They came up with some innovative ideas and we were very impressed with what they would be able to do for us in the future," then the decision makers are probably goal-oriented. If the answer is, "We were having some delivery problems and we needed someone else as backup," the decision process is probably more problem-avoidance oriented.

If the decision maker is extremely goal oriented you can check the extreme versus the moderate goal-orientation by how many other choices have been made similarly in terms of jumping to a new supplier or taking a risk to improve operations. Then you focus much more on finding out what that customer's most highly valued criteria are in terms of what he or she truly wants in that business context and personally, since the two most often will dovetail to some degree.

If the person is much more problem-avoidance oriented, then you first ascertain the worst problems to avoid, and then probe the dissatisfactions with the current suppliers. Direct confrontive questions such as, "Well, what's the worst thing about those who are supplying you right now?" will very often draw stereotyped answers such as, "There's nothing wrong. We're 100 percent happy with them. They're the greatest people on earth." So the first probe point is to question whether or not they are indeed satisfied. Do that very gently.

If they say they are 100 percent satisfied you can know in your heart of hearts that nobody's 100 percent satisfied with anything. So, a moment or two later, after other discussion, you might ask, "Since nobody bats 1.000, what are some of the areas you wish your current suppliers would improve upon?

You might get the response, "I can't think of anything."

"That's fine. I often can't either, right away," you might say. "But, if there were something, what would be its general direction?" If you're friendly and in rhythm and harmony with the prospect, he might say something like, "Well, of course, there are always concerns with delivery." Or, "Sometimes a price will jump and they didn't really call ahead of time to warn us. That's created a problem once or twice." When you get to this point you know you are on track to find out the irritants that that client may wish to avoid.

However, be careful and pay close attention to your prospect's reactions. Probe questions that aren't modified by your sensory acuity in noticing feedback cues can lead you to break rapport by being seen as overly pushy and not sensitive to the prospect's needs.

THE SEQUENTIAL/RANDOM SORT

Another useful piece of information when selling is knowing whether your customer sorts sequentially or randomly. Sequential sorters tend to be by-the-bookers. They like rules, protocols, procedures and shoulds. They like to approach their buying in a systematic manner. This system is so well defined to them that a salesperson who does not pick up on it will rapidly lose rapport and credibility.

A client of ours was entertaining a highly sequential sorter during lunch. The salesperson worked for a small Southern company that had a rule against having alcoholic beverages with clients – not even a glass of wine. The client's sequence of an ideal business lunch had the following pattern: a cocktail with non-business small talk, lunch while discussing details of the presentation, and closing the agreement during dessert.

What our client found as she tried to move from small talk to business, her sequential sorter would not move on, and thus remained at the small-talk level throughout lunch and dessert.

Two weeks later our client violated company rules and at their second business meeting had a glass of wine prior to lunch. This time the sequence moved along quite smoothly, and she was able to close the sale during dessert.

Now, how did she know what his sequence was? Fact-finding. Before calling on this client she spoke with two of the salesmen who had called on and sold this client before. Both had outlined their success sequences, and both had kiddingly asked her if she was good enough to sell him out of his sequential comfort zone.

If you tend toward sequential sorting you probably have a fairly well established presentation sequence. And when you encounter a random sorter it may seem as though he or she is all over the place, interrupting your presentation to ask off-the-wall, out-of-sequence questions.

Random sorters are very often the people who want to go off to have a cup of coffee to discuss an idea or suggest going out on their boat to discuss your presentation.

Random sorters often go off on their own tangents, and seemingly have less regard for time constraints than their sequentially-sorting counterparts.

Random sorters especially enjoy bouncing creative ideas around, making new connections and insights.

Trying to force a highly random sorting client into a rigid sequence or procedure will most likely irritate and bore him into dismissing you and your plan, just as he dismisses your rigid procedures.

"Go with the flow" is the key to selling these people.

THE COST/CONVENIENCE SORT

Recently associates from Holland visited us on their first trip to Florida. While driving them from the airport we swung through a drive-thru convenience store to pick up a bottle of orange juice. As we were driving away with our orange juice the Dutch couple expressed amazement at the lengths Americans go to in order to sell convenience. Indeed, we had paid a premium for the convenience of purchasing the pre-prepared, bottled orange juice without even leaving our car.

Our unconscious cost-versus convenience purchase decisions are all around us, from microwave meals to pre-buttered garlic bread. These decisions include tailors and barbers who make office calls to pool services and lawn services, the concierge who takes care of all hotel needs to the taxi driver who finds that special out-of-the-way restaurant. We are constantly making cost-versus-convenience choices.

While it may seem that clients most often mention cost as their chief (or only) purchase-decision factor, the reality is that they could be anywhere on the cost/convenience continuum. It's therefore important to question and probe to discover from which direction they are primarily sorting. The rise in service business in the U.S. is testimony to the fact that not everyone is sorting for cost.

Car salespeople can further testify that while most people initially mention cost as their major choice factor, they usually have a list of convenience and comfort features that can quickly override the first-mentioned cost factors.

Peace of mind (freedom from worry) is a major convenience sort, as a friend of ours discovered a few years back when selling a large calendar order to a regional chain of furniture stores in the Northeast.

When he presented his calendar proposal to the marketing manager he was told that he was more than five thousand dollars higher than his competitor. Rather than cutting price, our friend probed about the quality of the other calendars and how they were liked by the stores' customers. All was fine in those categories. But as he probed about such service variables

as drop shipments, change of imprint charges, billing procedures and so on, he noticed the marketing manager fidget,
furrow his brow and tighten his lips a bit when stating that
there were "a few snags in some of those areas."

With this information our friend offered referrals, case
examples and logical assurances that he and his company
would make sure all such details were handled professionally
and personally with no loose ends, haggling or wrangling to be
concerned about.

Within the hour the $94,000 calendar order was his.

A variation of the cost/convenience sort is the tradeoff
between cost, time and quality. In fact, within the printing
business there's a saying: "Time, cost, or quality... pick any
two." Of course, the implication is that one cannot have all
three-quick delivery, low cost and high quality. Where these
three variables are simultaneously in play, the first step is to
prioritize the three.

A way of visually presenting this tradeoff was developed by
Florida entrepreneur John Morris in one of his construction
businesses. He calls it the Cost/Time/Quality triangle and it
looks like this:

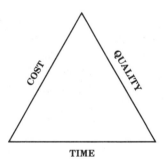

As John and his clients discuss potential projects and start
coming to a meeting of minds, he verbally questions them about

how they prioritize the three variables. As they move closer to agreement he actually discusses the triangle and its tradeoffs. As they approach final agreement he will actually draw and label the triangle and ask clients to place a dot in the triangle signifying where the project's emphasis should be. The most common variations are:

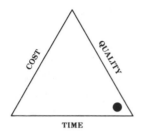

Want high quality in short amount of time while sacrificing low cost.

Want low cost and high quality in whatever time frame is available.

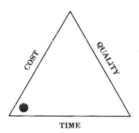

Want low cost and fast production while sacrificing quality.

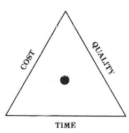

Attention to cost, time and quality in a way that provides good standards on all three, with neither extremely high nor extremely low levels on any of them.

John makes a point of keeping the drawing when agreement is reached and the client has drawn in the dot. If within the project the client starts changing priorities (e.g., "We need the work done two weeks earlier, but still within specifications and cost estimates"). John will calmly say, "OK, let's see how you'd like to move the dot."

This technique helps the client see the tradeoffs clearly, helps John avoid being victimized by whimsical priority changes and keeps the new negotiations on a cleaner, less personal level because of the already established acceptance of the model.

If your selling commonly includes this variation of the cost/convenience sort, you may wish to try this technique in some of your upcoming client discussions. When you do, you may be surprised at where within the triangle your client places the dot. While verbally the client indicates, "I'm interested in immediate, high quality service," the differences between the following placements will make a difference in what you finally offer.

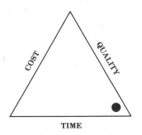

(i.e., cost is far secondary to immediacy and quality)

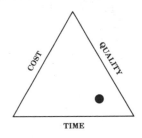

(i.e., cost is somewhat secondary to immediacy and quality)

THE BELIEVABILITY SORT

What makes you believe that a particular vacation resort is really good? Is it enough for someone you trust to tell you it's good, or do you have to see it? Or possibly you need to actually use it before you believe it's really good. How many times would you have to use it to know it was really good? Once? Twice? Three times? More? What about seeing it or its pictures? Once? Twice? More? Or how many trustworthy people telling you it is really good would it take to make you believe that resort is indeed really good? One? Two? More?

Remember our earlier discussion about visual, auditory and kinesthetic people? Most people are visual. That's probably why the saying, "seeing is believing" is so common to our language and our culture.

Others don't have to see the product or service at all to believe it's good. To them *word of mouth* advertising is best.

Still others don't really believe something is good until they involve themselves in it.

When you hear the old vacation question about going to the mountains or the seashore, what's your immediate response? Do you immediately go inside your head to one of those places? Do you see it? Hear it? Or feel its ambiance surrounding you? If it's a combination, which is first and which is strongest? Your answers to these questions should give you some insights regarding your believability sort for that decision.

When selling your product or service you encounter people who sort primarily in each of these ways - visually, auditorily or kinesthetically. These people also have either a number of times or a length of time it takes in their mode to truly believe something.

If you were selling copy machines, for example, a visual person may have to see copies from the machine to believe its quality. Within this group of visuals there's a fairly wide range of how many different types of copying examples it takes to effectively demonstrate the copier's quality. It's therefore important to be able to recognize how many examples such a person needs to be convinced.

If a customer needs multiple examples to be convinced, and you show only one or two examples, the believability factor will simply not be strong enough to motivate him toward buying. This person is sold easiest through being shown a variety of examples from one or a variety of machines.

The customer who is most comfortable relying on word of mouth endorsements also has a level at which the endorsements become believable. It may be from one trustworthy source, two, three or more. Falling short of that number when presenting testimonials will result in falling short of believability.

The customers who must use a copier to believe in it also have a threshold. It may be in numbers of times using the machine, or it may be length of time using it. Regardless, falling short of the threshold level will result in their not quite believing.

You've possibly noticed that there are a number of copier sales reps who are more than glad to place one of their copiers in your office on a trial basis for a month or so. Assuming it's a good machine, this believability strategy is beautiful because it allows the visuals to see multiple examples of the machine's quality, it provides the auditories multiple opportunities to discuss its attributes with other users in the company, and it allows those who want hands-on experience with it to play with the machine to their hearts' content.

So, as you've noticed, two different factors go into the believability sort. The first is which mode the buyer naturally sorts to, and the second, the number of times it takes to become believable.

ESTABLISHING CRITERIA

There is one overriding criteria-based question that is present in all selling situations. It is "what conditions must be met for us to do business?"

However, business protocol seldom allows the question to be asked so directly. Furthermore, the what-conditions-must-be-met-for-us-to-do-business question is probably too big a chunk for the client to answer completely and correctly even if he were inclined to do so. Therefore, needs-identification probes and questions are necessary.

Once the client's needs and sorting styles have been determined, *establishing criteria* is nothing more than prioritizing these needs so you respond first and best with the style that motivates the client most.

Remember the Time/Cost/Quality triangle mentioned earlier in this chapter? That triangle is a means of establishing a priority among those three variables. But in selling situations there are many more than three variables to identify and prioritize when establishing which criteria are most important to the client.

In the dialogue that follows, notice how specific qualifying questions can tell you much more about the buyer than what's on the surface. Let's consider selling a home to a single female bank auditor.

SALES ASSOCIATE: Hello, I'm Julie Martin.

CUSTOMER: Hello, I'm Margaret Brown of First State Bank. I was told by the people at my office that you have many listings in a five mile radius around our corporate office. I'm in the market to buy a home.

SALES ASSOCIATE: I'm glad they told you that good information, for we do have lots of listings in that part of town. Won't you sit down?

CUSTOMER: Thank you.

SALES ASSOCIATE: Tell me, Ms. Brown, what size home are you thinking about?

CUSTOMER: I'd like a two bedroom so that my mother can come and spend her vacations with me in comfort. She's 63 and visits about twice a year. I'd also like it to have a den because I often have work to do at home.

SALES ASSOCIATE: So it will be just you and occasionally your mother living there?

CUSTOMER: Yes. Also I travel often to audit our branch banks.

SALES ASSOCIATE: And you prefer the neighborhoods close to your corporate offices?

CUSTOMER: Yes. I've been told that that area has held its value quite well and is quite stable. And, I don't really trust condominiums because I've heard their quality is not up to par with more established neighborhoods and that their associations are always raising maintenance fees.

SALES ASSOCIATE: Do you have a specific price range in mind?

CUSTOMER: Oh yes. Based on the tables we use at the bank, as well as what the loan officers tell me, I need a home in the $85,000 to $89,000 range. With $30,000 down payment it would fit into my budget satisfactorily.

SALES ASSOCIATE: Good. Where are you living now?

CUSTOMER: Since I moved here two months ago, I've been renting a two-bedroom apartment down the street from the bank at 506 Oak Street on a month-to-month basis, and, frankly, I'd say I've been paying too much for the location.

SALES ASSOCIATE: I hear what you're saying. In the two months you've been here, have you had much chance to get familiar with the area?

CUSTOMER: Not firsthand, but I've talked with a number of my colleagues and they've told me of a couple of neighborhoods that sound just like where I grew up, and also sound as if they'll appraise within my budget.

SALES ASSOCIATE: What style house seems right for you?

CUSTOMER: I'd like another brick home, with a fireplace, that's located in a quiet neighborhood with very little traffic noise.

SALES ASSOCIATE: Have you done any house checking so far?

CUSTOMER: Not really. So far all I've done is consult with my colleagues, but now I'd say I'm ready.

SALES ASSOCIATE: I'm glad to hear that. What time frame are we talking about?

CUSTOMER: I'd like to start systematically checking this week. I've got three days of company time to find something, and I'm willing to spend some vacation days to make sure I find the best value for my money.

SALES ASSOCIATE: If we were to find a quiet two bedroom home with a fireplace and den that happened to be farther out, would that be acceptable if it were in your price range?

CUSTOMER: How far out?

SALES ASSOCIATE: Oh, say, eight or nine miles from your office.

CUSTOMER: Yes, if the other factors were to ring true.

SALES ASSOCIATE: Would that be preferable to paying a little more for something closer in, or not?

CUSTOMER: I have to tell you, if the figures don't fit we can't even discuss it.

SALES ASSOCIATE: I understand what you're saying. Is there anyone else you'll want to bring along to discuss the houses we visit?

CUSTOMER: I don't think so. I know what I want and if I have any reservations I've got several terrific experts at the office to discuss them with.

SALES ASSOCIATE: That's good to hear. Is this your first house purchase, or have you owned before?

CUSTOMER: It's actually my third home purchase. Before moving here from Memphis, I had my last house for three years. It just sold last month.

SALES ASSOCIATE: Tell me, how did you decide on the last house you owned?

CUSTOMER: Well, the situation was pretty similar to now. I was in an apartment and I talked to my colleagues for a couple months before deciding what I wanted. Then I visited a real estate agent that several of my associates recommended. Frankly, she wasn't very good and I wasted a lot of time looking at houses that I wouldn't really consider. When I told them she wasn't so good, my associates recommended another agent who was just great. He talked with me a long time until he understood exactly what I wanted. Then, even before going out to see them, we discussed their specifications, advantages and disadvantages. That saved a lot of time, because I could tell some of them were unsuitable just by discussing them. I'd say we only visited four or five homes before I was sure of my decision.

SALES ASSOCIATE: Did you take any of your associates along with you to see the houses?

CUSTOMER: No, not at all. But when I told them what I had found they were delighted for me and I signed the contract the next day.

Having read through this dialogue, how would you continue if you were the sales associate? Would you put her in the car and start visiting houses? We hope not. The customer has already made it clear that her buying strategy is to discuss a number of homes in the office before narrowing down the four or five houses to visit. She even quit a real estate salesperson who didn't recognize that.

Because we've contrived the dialogue to be short and a little more obvious than most discussions, you should be able to notice definite sorting patterns.

Use the Criteria Sorting Grid to indicate how you would read Margaret Brown, the customer. This will help you understand the concepts we've been explaining as well as learn to use the Criteria Sorting Grid as a customer-reading selling tool.

Here are the steps in using the Criteria Sorting Grid:

1. Go through each sorting group and check which subcategory is strongest for your customer. For example, Margaret Brown's main authority sort would be Others, so you'd check that.

Example:

☐ Authority Sort
_____ Self
__✓__ Others
_____ Data

2. Indicate how strong you think the major sort choice is. Since Margaret's pattern has a recurring theme of checking with her colleagues we'd score her pretty strong in her *Others* orientation. In the blank space between the subcategory and grid, you may wish to jot a note about who the *Others* are, for future reference.

Example:

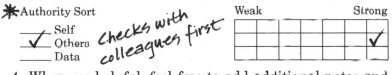

3. After completing both steps for all sorting categories, prioritize which are most important and least important. You can do this by simply starring those that are very important to use, checking those that are somewhat important and leaving the less important sorts blank. Since Margaret's *Others* orientation was so strong in comparison with the other sorts, we'd star her Authority Sort as a significant category to acknowledge and attend to.

✱Authority Sort   Weak   Strong
_____ Self   *checks with*
__✓__ Others   *colleagues first*
_____ Data

4. Wherever helpful, feel free to add additional notes and mental prompters that will later help you recall specifics about the customer you have interviewed.

Now, with this information take a look at the entire Criteria Sorting Grid (Figure 3.1) and rate how you would categorize and prioritize Margaret's sorting patterns. Do that now and then compare your evaluation with what we've done in Figure 3.2.

Finished? How did you do? The checks, stars and comments need not match exactly for you to have done it very well.

But we would expect your thinking and comments to be in the general direction of what's presented here.

To sell Margaret most effectively we would first talk to her a lot, listening carefully to her predispositions and needs. Then we would clarify these points to make certain we were hearing her correctly. We would probe with questions about what her colleagues had to say about certain points (e.g., neighborhoods, roads, shopping areas) and even offer to meet with her colleagues to discuss the pros and cons of any unresolved issues. (Remember, it's her colleagues she turns to for such guidance, so even the offer to talk with them or suggestion that she may wish to talk with them will build credibility and trust by fitting into her pattern.)

We would next suggest a way to approach the narrowing down process systematically while tuning in to as many of her specific points as possible. Since she has already commented on narrowing down the field to just a few houses before looking at any, we'd suggest a sequence that allowed for that—possibly going through the listings in the office and discussing their pros and cons.

Contrary to how we would treat many other home buyers, we would probably only show her listings of homes in her price range, not going above without her invitation or suggestion.

Her indications of liking what she's used to and liking neighborhoods with a stable background would lead us to work toward those goals, but we'd be willing to adjust in the face of price barriers or bad reviews from her colleagues.

Since she has indicated no particularly strong problem-avoidance patterns (beyond avoiding condo associations and their price raising politics) and has shared no strong goal orientation, we'd diminish the importance of that sort in our approach with her.

Let's try another one with different sorts and different needs. This person is a successful concert promoter. He's

CRITERIA SORTING GRID

Customer _____ _____   Company _____
                                     Sales Rep _____
                                     Date _____

Prioritize   Weak   Strong

Sorts

☐ Authority Sort

_____ Self
_____ Others
_____ Data

☐ Mismatch/Match Sort

_____ Mismatch Counter-example
_____ Mismatch Polarity
_____ Match

☐ General/Specific Sort

_____ General
_____ Specific

☐ Past Assurances/Future Possibilities Sort

_____ Past Assurances
_____ Future Possibilities

☐ Problem Avoidance/Goal Orientation Sort

_____ Problem Avoidance
_____ Goal Orientation

☐ Sequential/Random Sort

_____ Sequential
_____ Random

☐ Cost/Convenience Sort

_____ Cost
_____ Convenience
_____ (a) Time
_____ (b) Quality

☐ Believability Sort

_____ Visual
_____ Auditory
_____ Kinesthetic

How many times? or How long? _____

Figure 3.1

wealthy and seems preoccupied with things other than the real estate buying task at hand. The meeting is at his office.

SALES ASSOCIATE: Mr. Smithwick? I'm pleased to meet you face to face. I'm Steve Reynolds.

CUSTOMER: Yeah Steve, sure, sit down, and call me Bruce, would ya? Hey, you look like you could use a drink. What'll it be?

SALES ASSOCIATE: Thanks, I'll have the same thing you're having.

CUSTOMER: OK, I'll get 'em... Here you go.

SALES ASSOCIATE: Thanks.

CUSTOMER: Now, what do you have to show me?

SALES ASSOCIATE: What size house would you like to see?

CUSTOMER: Man, a *big* one. A party house. You know, one of those big places where everyone goes for a good time. Pool. Hot tub. Lots of bedrooms to crash in. You know. One of those big good-looking party houses where I can show my people a good time.

SALES ASSOCIATE: When you say lots of bedrooms, do you mean five, six or more?

CUSTOMER: More. I mean a big house. Maybe one overlooking the water. And secluded. Sometimes my friends don't want to be hassled, you know?

SALES ASSOCIATE: Sure. I know. What else would you like to see in it?

CUSTOMER: Hell, I don't know. I'm a promoter, you're the real estate man. You fill in the details!

SALES ASSOCIATE: Is there a particular price range you're looking at?

CUSTOMER: It depends on what you show me, but we're lookin' at seven digits anyhow. But it has to be something real special and within a half hour of the airport by limo. And I don't want something that was built for some geek who was 60 years old. I want it special.

CRITERIA SORTING GRID

Customer **Margaret Brown**

Company **First State Bank**
Sales Rep **Julie Brown**
Date _____

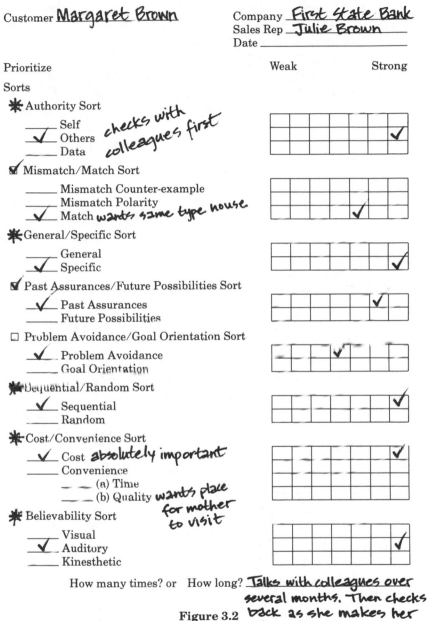

Prioritize   Weak   Strong

Sorts

✳ Authority Sort

_____ Self   *checks with*
✓ Others   *colleagues first*
_____ Data

☑ Mismatch/Match Sort

_____ Mismatch Counter-example
_____ Mismatch Polarity
✓ Match *wants same type house*

✳ General/Specific Sort

_____ General
✓ Specific

☑ Past Assurances/Future Possibilities Sort

✓ Past Assurances
_____ Future Possibilities

☐ Problem Avoidance/Goal Orientation Sort

✓ Problem Avoidance
_____ Goal Orientation

✳ Sequential/Random Sort

✓ Sequential
_____ Random

✳ Cost/Convenience Sort

✓ Cost *absolutely important*
_____ Convenience
_____ (a) Time
_____ (b) Quality *wants place for mother to visit*

✳ Believability Sort

_____ Visual
✓ Auditory
_____ Kinesthetic

How many times? or   How long? *Talks with colleagues over several months. Then checks back as she makes her decision.*

Figure 3.2

SALES ASSOCIATE: Special. That's good. Are there any houses you've seen lately with these "special" qualities you're talking about?

CUSTOMER: No. If I had I wouldn't need you.

SALES ASSOCIATE: Where are you living now?

CUSTOMER: Oh, I'm in the Biltmore Towers in the penthouse. When I saw the view I had to have it, even though it took me months to renovate it to my standards.

SALES ASSOCIATE: But now you're ready for something else.

CUSTOMER: Oh, I'll keep it for weeknights, but for living it's just too small for good entertaining and getting away for fun. I see my new house as a place to lay back and close deals. That's why it's got to be something special.

SALES ASSOCIATE: So it's not just for partying?

CUSTOMER: Partying is my business. It's all entertainment, it's all glamour and it's all work. That's why we call it show business. Now, are you going to sit here and talk all day or are you going to show me something?

SALES ASSOCIATE: Oh, I'm going to show you some real special homes, and they're going to be expensive. When we find your house, are you ready to move on it quickly?

CUSTOMER: You show me what I want and I'll move on it.

SALES ASSOCIATE: Good. By the way, what have you looked at so far?

CUSTOMER: Nothing. Just friends' places.

Based on this dialogue, how would you rate Bruce Smithwick? Use the blank Criteria Sorting Grid that follows to make your choices. Then check your answers against our rating sheet. Do that now.

Finished?

All right, let's analyze how to sell Bruce Smithwick. Without the skills you've already learned it would be easy to falsely conclude that a concert promoter would have lots of audio-related needs – e.g., a place with a prewired sound system, great acoustics, etc. Such is not the case here. Smithwick is definitely a visual person. Plus, as indicated on the sheet, he seems to get feelings from what he sees that let him know something is right. It also appears that such feelings come immediately. If it's right for him he knows it on the spot and will act upon it.

His authority sort is strongly self. *He* knows what *he* wants when *he* sees it. His tendency to be somewhat of a mismatcher further emphasizes that here is a person who probably is hard to sell, but who buys quite easily.

It's good to know that people who are strong self sorters and who mismatch with counter-examples or polarity responses are particularly inclined to challenge you with prove-it-to-me statements that can spiral you into a pointless matching of wits. In such cases a good strategy is to counter with, "You are so good at knowing your needs that only you can truly decide what's ultimately right." When you encounter such sorters be aware of this possibility.

Since Smithwick is a general sorter, you would want to keep details at a minimum and work as quickly as possible toward the bottom line of which criteria he holds as most important. Even if you don't find exactly what he wants, his future possibilities sort tells you he may be willing to take something he can shape into his own image.

If a place approximates what he wants you'd prepare him with statements such as, "With your great eye you can see how this could be converted to..." Why? Because he probably can. Remember how he changed his penthouse. Also, replaying his "party house" images will give momentum to his future possibilities sort as he considers what could be.

He is not someone who will likely quibble over price once he has found what he wants.

Because he sorts randomly he's likely to be difficult to keep on task without pandering to his goal of getting just what he wants.

CRITERIA SORTING GRID

Customer _____   Company _____
                                      Sales Rep _____
                                      Date _____

Prioritize   Weak   Strong

Sorts

☐ Authority Sort

_____ Self
_____ Others
_____ Data

☐ Mismatch/Match Sort

_____ Mismatch Counter-example
_____ Mismatch Polarity
_____ Match

☐ General/Specific Sort

_____ General
_____ Specific

☐ Past Assurances/Future Possibilities Sort

_____ Past Assurances
_____ Future Possibilities

☐ Problem Avoidance/Goal Orientation Sort

_____ Problem Avoidance
_____ Goal Orientation

☐ Sequential/Random Sort

_____ Sequential
_____ Random

☐ Cost/Convenience Sort

_____ Cost
_____ Convenience
        _____ (a) Time
        _____ (b) Quality

☐ Believability Sort

_____ Visual
_____ Auditory
_____ Kinesthetic

How many times? or How long? _____

Figure 3.3

CRITERIA SORTING GRID

Customer **Bruce Smithwick** Company **Smithwick Promotions**
Sales Rep **Steve Reynolds**
Date _____

Prioritize   Weak   Strong

Sorts

✳ Authority Sort

  ✓ Self

  ____ Others

  ____ Data

Weak					Strong
					✓

☐ Mismatch/Match Sort

  ✓ Mismatch Counter-example

  ____ Mismatch Polarity

  ____ Match

Weak					Strong
			✓		

☐ General/Specific Sort

  ✓ General

  ____ Specific

Weak					Strong
				✓	

✳ Past Assurances/Future Possibilities Sort

  ____ Past Assurances

  ✓ Future Possibilities

Weak					Strong
					✓

☐ Problem Avoidance/Goal Orientation Sort

  ____ Problem Avoidance

  ✓ Goal Orientation

Weak					Strong
				✓	

☐ Sequential/Random Sort

  ____ Sequential

  ✓ Random

Weak					Strong
				✓	

☐ Cost/Convenience Sort

  ____ Cost

  ✓ Convenience *Wants to move now. Needs 30 min. to air-*

    ✓ (a) Time

    ✓ (b) Quality *port. Wants*

✳ Believability Sort *party place with great view.*

  ✓ Visual *"know it when I see it"*

  ____ Auditory *Also wants particular*

  ____ Kinesthetic *feel - no hassle -*

Weak					Strong
					✓

How many times? or How long? **Will move quickly when he sees what he wants. (e.g., "When I saw the view I had to have it.")**

Figure 3.4

QUESTIONS AND ANSWERS

Question: *Can understanding someone's sorting patterns make me an instant closer?*

Answer: At this point closing is not the issue. While it is possible to close a sale by manipulating people through their sorting patterns, it's not recommended for at least two major reasons. One reason is that the inevitable buyer remorse will be much greater and will often lead to order cancellation and/or no additional business from the customer. After all, who wants to feel "had?" A second reason is that if needs are identified and criteria are prioritized effectively, the sale can usually be completed with a minimum amount of buyer remorse and a maximum amount of buyer/seller satisfaction.

At a minimum, matching a person's sorting patterns will keep you from swimming against the strong tidal current of his or her basic buying inclinations. Indeed, once you are flowing within your customer's basic sorting patterns you'll find your sales momentum increasing as you speak.

Question: *It sounds as though utilizing sorting patterns is yet another way of establishing rapport.*

Answer: It is definitely a method of increasing rapport because it helps you more easily communicate within another person's model of reality. In this way you in essence are adding a turbo charge to the high powered pacing skills you learned earlier.

This combination is not only effective in selling contexts; it can greatly improve your level of rapport and persuasiveness with colleagues, friends, family and other loved ones.

Consider how much smoother family discussions would run if the questions and suggestions were paced and framed in one another's sorting patterns. In fact, you may wish to use the Criteria Sorting Grid to analyze others outside your sales arena.

Sorting patterns can even extend to how you motivate yourself. Try plugging yourself into the Criteria Sorting Grid and note where your personal priorities lie. Then consider some outcome you desire that may require some selling to yourself. Make sure your outcome matches what you *really* want so you don't end up selling yourself on something dysfunctional to your overall personal success definition. Then map out a sales script for yourself, paying close attention to your personal needs and criteria. It's a great way to get more personally motivated. To stay motivated, review your personal sales script daily, reaffirming your outcome and congratulating yourself on your daily progress.

As with selling your customers, if your personal selling script matches your personal sorting criteria and outcomes, your job will be much easier. For example, if you happen to be more problem avoidance oriented than goal oriented, but still wish to increase your income by 50%, you'll sell yourself more effectively by focusing on the problems you can and will avoid by achieving the volume necessary for a 50% increase. In doing that, the goal actually remains the same, but the motivating force behind it is strengthened.

Question: *Do people's sorting patterns remain the same in every situation?*

Answer: Not exactly. Individuals do tend to sort in the same ways pretty consistently. But their needs and therefore their short-term priorities change. For example, a business person who sorts toward the goal orientation of maximizing profits may often take a short-term cash-flow problem-avoidance approach, sacrificing some eventual profits to assure smoother passage to his long-term goal. In toward-versus-away terms it would be the idea of retreating in battle to eventually win the war.

It is, therefore, important to recognize your customer's basic sorting patterns, but realize that they may well appear to vary as their priorities change. So always recheck.

The stronger and more highly prioritized the person's sorting pattern, the more consistently he will stay in pattern.

Question: *Are these the only sorting patterns or are there more?*

Answer: There are more. Many more. What we've included here are sorting patterns that are most useful in most selling contexts. Others might include that some people perceive facets of their world in basically positive terms, and some in basically negative terms. We're sure you've encountered both extremes.

Some people have an interesting sorting pattern that tells them expensive is best (probably because they equate it with quality). These people will not buy if your product or service is underpriced.

Some people typically need lots of others around to enjoy themselves, some need a few, some need one, and some typically enjoy being alone—yet another way of sorting that probably would be of little use to your selling skills unless you are selling vacation retreats or some other form of lifestyle.

Think about your selling situations in terms of sorting patterns. Are there any high-priority ones that you typically encounter that are not already on our Criteria Sorting Grid? In seminars we help clients identify these patterns that are peculiar to their selling situations. Here we'd like you to stretch for at least one to add to the bottom of the Criteria Sorting Grid to tailor it more closely to your needs.

With this accomplished we're ready to advance to harnessing your client's objectives.

CHAPTER FOUR

Harnessing Objectives, Checking Rapport and Offering the Plan

HARNESSING OBJECTIVES

By the time you are ready to harness your client's objectives, you already will have gained rapport, identified the needs, established the criteria by which that person will make purchase decisions, and figured out the pattern of that person's convincer strategies. By this point, you already have most of the who, what, where, when, why and how raw materials to work with. Now you need to prioritize them so you understand which are the most important needs, which are the most highly valued criteria, and which strategies are the most likely to be used in making the purchase decisions.

If you've asked your questions well in the identification of needs and the establishing of criteria, you probably already have a very good intuitive feel for the priorities in your client's mind. However, you still check them out. The first stage of checking them out may certainly be to ask directly, "What are our priorities in developing your needs?" Or, "What are the most important needs we should respond to first?" This type of information is important in case you encounter conflicting goals or tradeoffs.

Often, a low-priority item may have the ability to reject a plan without particularly enhancing it. For example, third or fourth on the list, a person may say, "Oh yes, and we have to have delivery by December 1." If there are many choices that can be delivered by December 1, then December 1 is only a rejection point. It isn't an enhancement point. The fewer the choices, however, the more December 1 moves up in the priority list. Someone needing something for his or her grand opening that is approximately 72 hours away may indeed find that delivery is a number one priority and other choices, such as price and packaging, are far secondary to that need.

Similarly, we sometimes have one-way convincer strategies. For example, a critic can squelch a movie and keep us from going to it by the review. But assuming it gets a good rating, we may still require talking to several other people and getting their opinions on it before we actually go. Or, if the CEO likes the particular strategic direction, we may investigate strategy alternatives in that direction. But if the boss doesn't, then it shuts down that particular direction. So, on every level of needs, criteria and strategies, we learn which pieces are crucial and which pieces are not crucial—what's required versus what would be nice to have.

When we speak of harnessing objectives the metaphoric image we wish to instill is that of a team of horses harnessed together and galloping in the same direction. This direction should be along a well established roadway of how the customer and the company most commonly and comfortably make decisions. Then we want to attach our plan and our ideas to that team that is galloping towards success down the pre-established path. So harnessing objectives means first, lining up the key needs with the greatest needs and the greatest benefits leading them all. We present these outcomes to make sure that we understand what the client really wants. As we present them we also add the question, "And what else might be important?"

When we're fairly certain we have all the key variables, we're ready to build momentum by having lined up all our objectives and gotten them all galloping in the same direction in the same cadence and rhythm that our client likes to see, hear, and feel.

The presentation of these harnessed objectives is a well orchestrated preplay of the outcomes and the benefits to be had. This is more than acknowledging the objectives your client has in mind. It's actually getting enthused about these objectives. It's buying into them, empathizing, feeling and amplifying the surge of success that your client must be wishing or longing for.

Harnessing the objectives, therefore, means that you are preplaying the outcomes that your client wants in such a manner that your client feels that you not only understand and accept these outcomes as important, but also empathize and desire them too.

At this stage you may not yet have any answers. All you are agreeing on at this point are the questions, the direction and the desired result. Be careful here not to prematurely try to force what the client is saying into your preconceived idea of what you came to sell. Hear your client out to such an extent that when you play out your description of the client's objectives in your own words you can see the client light up, start nodding and say, "Yes, that's right." Listen for the firmness in the tonality that stresses yes, you're truly on target. Sense the good feelings that come from two people being in agreement as to what they want.

By the time you have harnessed objectives and presented them to your client in an effective manner, you should truly have answered the question, "What conditions must be met for us to do business with that client?"

When presenting these objectives to your client, realize that the benefit package is for both of you. For you it will save lots of time in that it will keep you from having to run in the wrong direction based on miscues, poor assumptions, and lack of data. For example, if a major criterion is that the price must be within a particular dollar range or else the plan won't fly, you'll save lots of time by not investigating those alternatives that exceed the budget. On your client's side, you have a real opportunity to amplify as well as clarify your client's personal needs and objectives. If you present them in a form where the clients experience the payoff as if it has already happened, then you are also building a certain level of commitment to the plan that you are going to bring back even before the plan is formed. For example, you may present it in this fashion: "Mrs. Johnson, if I understand correctly, you are looking for executive gifts in the $25 range that will go in an executive's office, will carry your logo, and can also be personalized. You want something that they probably have not had before, but that they would definitely appreciate. So it should be something unique and in good taste with delivery by December 1. I understand. It should arrive gift boxed and in good shipping cartons for safe mailing. You also want this well chosen gift to match your corporate identity and align with the trade advertising you've been using throughout the year. So, what you'd like is for me to bring only suggestions that match these criteria. Is that correct?"

If indeed you have hit most of Mrs. Johnson's criteria, you'll sense it in her mannerisms, such as good or better eye contact. When she agrees with you, "Yes, that's what I'm looking for," you'll hear that resoluteness in her voice. If any of these are missing, then go back and probe a little bit, questioning, "Is there something else we need to consider?"

If Mrs. Johnson has also mentioned to you that the way she knows a gift was successful is that she gets lots of thank you letters for it from the clients, then build that into your presentation of the objectives by saying, "And you want something that's so special and appropriate that dozens of your clients will respond with personal thank you notes. Is that right?" She'll agree, yes, if that's what she told you. And then you'll smile and say, "I believe that I can help you in this matter."

In harnessing the objectives we cannot overemphasize the importance of using the client's own words and phrases, the client's own objectives in her own tonality, in her own speech pattern, even with her own style of gestures.

If you harness the objectives optimally, you will already have momentum toward your plan before your plan is even formed. The environment in which your plan is offered will then be so enriched by good preparation that the resistance most salespeople get will not be a factor for you.

At this point, we have covered the steps of GRIN and ECHO—which are Gain Rapport, Identify Needs, Establish Criteria and Harness Objectives. In many types of selling this is as far as the initial contact goes, because many salespeople at this point go back to their offices and come up with a plan. In many other types of selling, however, the next steps follow immediately.

CHECK RAPPORT

CROP, you'll recall, stands for Check Rapport and Offer Plan. Regardless of whether you continue on in one sales presentation and move straight to check rapport and offer the plan, or you leave and come back, the Check Rapport step is still important.

Consider the "check rapport" step to be a safeguard. As you reconsider the continuum between pacing and leading you'll recognize that by the time you check rapport, you're getting ready to take more and more of the lead.

If you've had to leave and come back to the client, checking rapport becomes even more essential because you will have lost momentum in the time you were gone, be it hours, days, weeks or longer. It would also be a good idea at this point to review your Criteria Grid Manual before facing your client. This preparation will get you in much quicker rapport.

If you find you have rapport and you are in rhythm and harmony with your client, both physically and in terms of outcomes, then you can move forward after a quick recap. The quick recap will entail those agreements you've already established—the needs and criteria that you outlined with your client, and the objectives that you've agreed upon. As you review pacing the client's words, tones, body language, etc., you'll notice the client quickly getting back to that anticipatory level she had when you harnessed the objectives.

Rather than trust your feelings, check your rapport in a sensory specific manner also. For example, when you feel you are in rapport with your client and you notice that the two of you are sitting in approximately the same manner, shift your position and see if the client unconsciously follows. If the two of you are sitting cross-legged, when you feel you are in rapport uncross your legs and change positions slightly. If your client follows, you have a clear signal that you are moving from the pacing to the leading. You can do the same in terms of voice modulation as you talk. You may switch from projecting enthusiastically to softer tones. If indeed your client's voice in response to yours drops down a little more softly too, then the two of you are in harmony. You are truly at the pacing-to-leading cusp.

Sometimes upon checking rapport you'll find you no longer have it. For example, you may return to find the whole tone of the office has changed. In such cases you start at the Gain Rapport level and use all of the pacing strategies. You'll also re-identify needs, to find out what needs have changed and what else of significance has happened since you were there before. Since the criteria have possibly changed, you then make certain you still agree on the criteria and objectives that you established earlier. You may want to use your client's Criteria Grid Sheet on a point-by-point basis.

At this point, you either should have gained rapport or you should have a feeling for why that rapport has changed. Has more information changed the level of rapport you initially had? Has a key variable been changed, such as the budget? Is the person simply having a bad day? Whatever the changes, be aware of them before you advance further.

If on that sales call you find the client is in no way receptive to hearing your plan, you need to respect that. In most circumstances, the inconvenience that change causes you will be far outweighed in the heightened receptiveness your client will have toward you when you two finally are able to get back together and get down to business. This is not to say that you need to run out the door immediately. Make sure you understand what the game is before you develop your strategy as how to play it.

Only when you have rapport should you offer your plan. Why? Because offering a great plan in an environment of low trust and low rapport is analogous to throwing very good seeds on concrete. No matter how good the seeds are, the infertility of their surroundings will prevent them from taking hold, growing and flourishing. Use your sensory acuity and stay flexible.

The more you develop your sensory acuity, the more important you will realize it is. Within social situations, as well as in business, you will begin noticing subtle differences in how people respond to different ideas and how they respond to different people. You will notice such things in your work and recreation schedule. You will find yourself cross-referencing what you've learned here with what you're experiencing out there and you'll start weaving it in more and more.

One byproduct of such sensory acuity was reported to us by a seminar participant as a result of his weekly poker game. Using his newly gained attention to sensory details, he noticed that one of his weekly poker buddies had developed an unconscious habit of placing his poker chips on the table in a slightly different manner when he was bluffing than when he was making a normal bet. This very subtle difference was tested out by calling the bluffs. In reporting this to us, our participant could hardly keep a straight face at the thought of how many poker hands this one piece of sensory information could win him over the years. Now that he has learned to read these small sensory differences he says, "My poker buddy might as well have a red light flashing 'bluff' every time he tries it on me from this point on."

Practice and you will be amazed at the wealth of information you'll pick up from people's unconscious gestures just by using your senses and paying attention to subtle changes in how they communicate with you.

LACKING T-H-E M-A-N

If you find your level of rapport lacking in terms of feeling comfortable with advancing to the plan-offering stage, you may wish to analyze the situation as to whether or not your customer is lacking T-H-E M-A-N. These initials stand for your customer lacking:

Trust
Hurry
Empathy (for you)

Money
Authority
Need (for what you are selling)

Lack of Trust

If trust is what is lacking, then return to your Criteria Grid Worksheet and make sure you have the proper fix on his believability sort. Then add evidence of your ability to provide the needed benefits in the customer's believability sorting pattern. For example, if your prospect needs to see three proofs before a new idea is believable, show him at least three letters from satisfied customers, or three or more published articles extolling the virtues of your product or service. If your prospect needs to *hear* the proofs, offering a client list of satisfied customers he may call will serve you better. If trust is lacking, chances are either you did not utilize the customer's pattern originally, or your examples were not perceived as legitimate or real. Unreferenced statistics and quotes often fall into the latter category.

Lack of Hurry

If your customer experiences little hurry or urgency to own what you are selling, your plan is in danger of being placed on the back burner. A few years ago my wife and I were interested in a security system for our home, even though our neighborhood is quite safe and there was no indication that the status of our home or safety would change in the foreseeable future.

The salesman was simply in our home to provide us with information for whenever we did decide we wanted a system installed. Again, there was no hurry whatsoever. We had lived in our home for six years quite safely without such a system.

By the time the salesman had checked our house, the number of entrance ways, the number of places for high-tech scanners and the best place for central controls, he had thoroughly qualified us, understood our needs and our lack of concern for our immediate security.

He demonstrated his product, showed us several articles regarding their state-of-the-art equipment, endorsements, specifications and independent laboratory evaluations comparing their units with their competitor's. (He had shown me what I needed to know in terms of my believability sort.)

Additionally, at my wife's request he supplied us with the names of five different people in our general area who had installed such a system within the last two years and had given permission to have future prospects call them to ask their level of satisfaction with the system. (Her believability sort.)

Even so, there was no hurry, at least not until he told the story of one of his commercial clients. They had their system installed and were struck by burglars that very evening—even before they bothered to stick their security decals on their doors and windows. Of course, the criminals were caught, and the jewelry store owners were so glad the burglars had not struck the night before. He also added (somewhat heavy-handedly, I thought) how much it would bother him if one of his customers were burglarized while simply waiting to do what they knew they were going to do eventually.

Then came the question, "By the way, are you folks going on vacation this summer?" We were leaving for Europe in three weeks. Suddenly, I wasn't buying a security system. I was buying additional peace of mind and enjoyment on my vacation. My wife called three of the references the next day and the system was installed the following week. The vacation was wonderful.

Lack of Empathy

Empathy is emotional identification. It's *feeling with*. If the customer is not empathizing with you, the problem and solution lie in your handling of the basic rapport skills covered in the rapport section of this book.

If you're not receiving the empathy level you need, you can improve the situation by improving one or more of your emotional pacing, agreement pacing, posture pacing, tone and tempo pacing, language pacing, values and beliefs pacing, cultural pacing, content pacing, or interest pacing.

The point here is that we get what we give. Customers empathize with us when we are in rapport with them. The outward demonstrations of rapport are the pacing skills mentioned above.

Lack of Money

There's an old Las Vegas joke about a harried looking businessman with two days of stubble who approaches a stranger outside one of the casinos and begs, "Could you please spare me a few extra dollars? My wife and kids are with me and we don't have any money for food or for a place to stay. Any amount will help. Please!"

The stranger responded by asking, "If I were to give you some money, how do I know that you simply won't take the money, go inside and gamble it away?"

The distraught man looked at the stranger indignantly, pulled out a wad of twenties and exclaimed, "Gambling money I've got!"

In nearly all selling situations there is money for what is wanted badly enough. Most of the time when a customer professes to lack the money to purchase a product or service, the situation can be translated to mean, "I am not yet ready to trade my big stack of money for that little stack of potential value that you have demonstrated so far."

Rare is the sales professional who has not been greeted at the door with the comment, "I'll talk with you, but I'll tell you right now we don't have any budget for what you're going to show me."

In such situations it's best to proceed as if there is money, and be sure to check their credit.

Lack of Authority

Some estimates are that nearly two out of three sales calls are made on people with insufficient authority to make the buying decision by themselves. Often they have the authority to say no, but not the authority to say yes (by themselves).

After following the steps of gaining rapport, identifying needs, establishing criteria, and harnessing objectives you have done enough fact-finding to effectively offer your plan, providing you are talking to a decision-maker. The problem is that if you are speaking to someone who has no authority or only partial authority to purchase, he or she may intentionally withhold this information unless you ask directly. Of course, asking directly, "Do you have authority to buy?" is a little blunt, and will often draw either irritation or lack of candor. Even so, this clarification point needs to be made before the actual plan is presented.

We generally subscribe to sales trainer Tom Hopkins' qualifying question (with some additional softeners added to make the question pass more smoothly): "Mr./Ms. New Prospect, if we were to be fortunate enough to find the right (whatever you're selling) today, would we be in a position to move forward right now, or are there some other people we would need to involve?"

Through using these "we's" and suggesting there might be "... some other people *we* would need to involve," we stand an improved chance of getting a straight answer if the person does not have full authority to buy.

In such a case the best scenario is to then move toward offering your plan to both the person in front of you and the person who holds the buying power. A major key is to build an alliance that will allow you to sell to the decision-maker while allowing your initial contact to look and feel good as a result of helping you.

Lack of Need

Sometimes prospects simply don't need what you are selling. But that's far less often than you probably think. First of all, needs and wants are not very different in our minds. Sure we need food, shelter and clothing, but do we need *that particular* food in our refrigerators, *that particular* residence, or *those particular* clothes?

We choose our food, home and clothes more in terms of satisfactions rather than actual needs. In fact, nearly everything we purchase has one or more satisfactions it provides for us.

Lack of need usually translates into lack of understanding of what the product or service can do for the customer that will be more desirable than having the money. Such desires might include the:

Desire to make money
Desire to save money
Desire for power
Desire for prestige
Desire for security
Desire for physical comfort
Desire for fewer interruptions
Desire for peace of mind
Desire for convenience
Desire for praise
Desire for professional recognition
Desire for family affection
Desire for good health

Desire for longevity
Desire for more responsibility
Desire for family togetherness
Desire for energy and vigor
Desire for information
Desire for more control
Desire for fun
Desire for personal growth
Desire for love
Desire to be remembered
Desire to be like people we admire
Desire to feel/appear unselfish or generous
Desire to avoid pain
Desire to avoid criticism
Desire to avoid the unknown
Desire to avoid responsibility
Desire to avoid failure
Desire to avoid looking foolish
Desire to avoid losing those things we are pleased to already possess
... and so on.

Lack of need on the part of the prospect too often translates to lack of innovative perception on the part of the salesperson. Looking beyond the obvious, past the probable, and all the way to the possible is the best answer here.

OFFER PLAN

In this section we will first describe the many powerful covert persuasion techniques that are often woven into sales presentations as well as an ethical foundation for thought. Then we'll look at the power of metaphors, analogies and stories and why they are so effective in selling. This will lead to strategies for getting the client further involved in your plan through utilizing projections and envisioning outcomes. The hypnotic effect of pattern talk will be presented as well as other patterns for generating agreement, such as the three persuasive ties and the stroke-and-lead technique. With all of these techniques and strategies in place we'll conclude with your overall framework for offering your plan, complete with a checklist of key points. Throughout this section, keep in mind that when you are selling at your best much of your persuasive power will be below your own conscious awareness. As you have possibly experienced from time to time, your words and actions will seem to flow naturally without conscious effort.

SEEING IS BELIEVING

A short while ago, several of us were on a pleasure cruise. As we were looking over the rail at the great expanse of sea that stretched farther than our eyes could carry us, we marveled at how much ocean there was out there.

"Yeah," quipped one of our group, "and that's only the top."

What's on the surface may be impressive enough, but what's going on below the surface is much greater and much more important. In a sense, that's how presentation skills are. Much of what we will talk about in this section relates to what goes on below the surface of conscious awareness.

THE POWER OF SUGGESTION

Clearly, one of the most important skills in presentations is the power of suggestion. For example, as you're reading these words quietly to yourself you may notice a growing need at the back portion of your tongue to swallow. As you notice yourself needing to swallow and going through the motion, you may wonder how we know so much about you.

Have you swallowed yet? Has that wonder crossed your mind yet? Give a slight smile and know it's true. Have you smiled yet?

What we've done here is nothing more than make several suggestions and hook them onto each other. Swallowing has no bearing on wondering how we know something about you. And certainly smiling has no bearing on knowing it's true. Yet, by simply suggesting something that can easily happen, we (brought it to your mind,) and most probably affected your behavior by suggesting it. Then, once having affected behavior on a small level, we added another suggestion that was somewhat more of a stretch. Had we simply started with, "You may wonder how we know so much about you," your immediate reaction may have been, "I see no proof you know anything about me at all." Then we took even a greater jump and suggested that noticing this may make you smile, and smiling would make you believe it. All of these are non-sequiturs. The only real connection among them is that we were suggesting that one leads to the other.

AVOID RAISING NEGATIVE POINTS

As we've discussed before, the word "not" in front of a suggestion or command won't remove the image, thought or feeling. For example, let us suggest that you *not* imagine a lemon or lime wedge with its tart, squirty acidic juices underneath the back of your tongue. We suggest you not imagine how that squirting underneath your tongue would make your mouth water. Let's suggest that you not let that image of squirting lemon and lime wedges affect your salivation right now.

As you notice salivation tendencies in your mouth you realize that the word "not" is ineffective at removing the suggestion. This understanding is extremely important in harnessing the power of suggestion and galloping in the direction you want.

Because suggestions are so incredibly powerful, care must be taken in how we use them, lest we misuse them and have them backfire on us. In using suggestions effectively we must always focus on what we want, instead of what we don't want. Many salespeople end up sabotaging buyer confidence by raising negative issues. For example, a salesperson may hear himself try to reinforce a close with words such as, "And I don't want you to worry about the quality of this product."

At that point he has unintentionally raised the worry of quality. How much that worry has been raised may well determine whether or not he gets the order. If this negative suggestion triggers some fear reactions with the client, and if the salesperson at that point does not have enough evidence that quality is not a problem, then the sale could be lost on that quality question.

Try this: Pretend you are peacefully asleep in your own warm bed, and the phone rings at two in the morning. As you sleepily answer the phone you hear the voice of a loved one saying, "Before I tell you what's happened, promise you won't panic!"

What are you going to do immediately? That's right, panic! Perhaps the next line is, "Our car's broken down. We're all right. There's a towing van coming, but we won't be home for another few hours." While that's good news, there still is a strong likelihood that your heart will continue to pound out of your chest. The panic reaction will still be hanging on, and you can bet this won't be one of those times that you can snuggle back in bed and fall right back to sleep.

How much better it would have been for the voice to have said, "We're all fine, but the car has broken down, and we won't be home for a couple more hours. We wanted you to sleep comfortably even though we're not home at the time you expected."

For that reason we need to be very careful using such suggestions as, "Don't spill your milk, don't miss, don't worry," or "Don't feel self-conscious, nobody is staring at you." At least we should avoid such words if our intent is to have them not do those things. If,on the other hand, you do want to raise doubt and concern, you can use those same expressions, but with different intent.

One of our clients who enjoys golf betting tells us that suggestions such as, "Don't slice it," "Pay attention to not hit that big water hazard," and "Be careful not to tighten up as you approach the ball" are commonly used to psyche out opponents.

In selling, the time to raise negative issues is only when they are to your advantage.

For example, the computer system you are selling has an internal, highly tested circuit breaker. This means that even if the external circuit breaker fails, the internal circuit breaker will stop surges in electricity from damaging the hardware or the software. Salespersons can raise this negative specter very effectively by either directly suggesting, "I don't want you to be concerned about an electric surge getting through your initial surge protector and damaging this machine." Then this must be immediately followed by, "Here is proof that this machine has the most sophisticated surge protector in the industry built right into the system." By using proof immediately, all competitors are left in doubt, but your particular computer is not.

A second way to raise the concern is with a question, such as, "Are you, by the way, concerned about electric surges damaging your hardware?" If the prospect says "Yes" then the proof should immediately follow. If the prospect says "No" the salesperson can explain the scenario of hardware being damaged by the surge that gets past the external surge protector and damages the equipment. Then he or she must show the proof or explain how this computer's internal surge protector is the best available. This strategy is a way of adding one more decision criterion to the decision process. It's best used when there's a problem-avoidance advantage that the competition cannot meet, and the buyer has not already considered the need to avoid the problem. When these two conditions are met, the negative issue strategy can be a major plus factor.

SUGGESTIONS OF CAUSE AND EFFECT

Now that you are beginning to understand the incredible power of embedding suggestions into the way you present, you are ready to understand just how they can establish a cause-and-effect relationship in your prospect's mind. There are three cause and effect linkage systems.

The first and the weakest is simply using the word "and." In this manner, "I see you are looking at our best samples *and* seeing the quality," or "I hope you enjoyed your meal *and* will tell your friends about us." A waitress might say, "I see you are finishing up your meal *and* are ready for dessert."

The second cause and effect linkage uses temporal words such as "when, as, while, and during," and in doing so establishes a connection in time. Here are some examples: "*As* you continue reading these materials, *you will* find yourself understanding more and more about how to improve your selling skills." Or, "*While* you are reading these materials *you'll probably find* yourself thinking of places you can try these new skills out." A person selling you a new suit might say, "*When* you try it on *you'll notice the feeling* of quality in the wearing."

The third and strongest linking is actually stating causality through your words. Words such as "causes, forces, requires, and makes" are used in this context. For example, "You may have noticed that applying these concepts *makes you want* to learn even more." To a client who is raising a lot of objections, a salesperson might comment, "I see asking the questions *helps* you make good purchase decisions." By combining the first and third linkages, a salesperson might say, "Why don't you have a seat *so* you can relax *and* enjoy the presentation?" Variations and combinations of these three types of linkages can be very powerful influences on how your customer, client, or prospect perceives what you are presenting.

Here are some more variations on these three approaches. "Why don't you sit over here and relax *so you can* make a good decision?" "Have you noticed how this home's environment *has caused you* to feel more comfortable?"

This last example brings us to the next level of embedding suggestions and commands. You are already aware that asking questions psychologically involves the other person in the question. When combining questions with embedded suggestions, you are able to make presuppositions that more easily guide the client in the appropriate direction. Awareness questions with words such as "realize, understand, know, noticed, aware" are ideal for presupposing the rest of the sentence. For example, "Are you aware that using our technique throughout the book has already helped you understand things better?" Or, "Have you noticed how well this car matches your personality?" "Do you realize we are much closer to agreement than we were a few minutes ago?"

EITHER-OR CHOICES

Questions using either-or choices are also good for presupposing that one or two or three variables will be selected. For example, "Would you prefer to select shoes *before or after* we choose the outfit?" "Would an appointment at three o'clock be all right, or would four-thirty be better?" To a couple browsing in a showroom a salesperson might comment, "We have such a wide selection I wonder which one of you will be the first to find something you really love?" What is presupposed is that one of them will find something he or she loves. The response the couple gives back will typically tell who is usually the initial decider. Pay attention to and respect such comments as her saying, "Well, he'll fall in love with it but I'm the one who has to decide if we can afford it." In such cases the buyers have told you who has the hair trigger on their emotions and who is most likely to hold back and try to make a cold decision. In such cases, sell emotionally and justify with logic. Why? Because in most cases that's how people buy. They find things that please them emotionally and they rationalize the rest of it.

ADVERB AND ADJECTIVE PRESUPPOSITIONS

Using adverbs and adjectives in questions can also be very effective in presupposing for the client. For example, "How *easily*, can you make a choice today?" While questioning how easily it's presupposed that a choice can be made today.

"How interested are you in improving your secretaries' productivity?" In this example, by questioning *how* interested, one presupposes that they are interested to some degree.

Questions that use time-related verbs and adverbs such as "already, yet, still, stop, start, continue, begin, anymore" are also good tools for embedding suggestion through presupposing. "Are you still interested in buying investment real estate?" is a question that presupposes that there has been interest. "When would you like to begin deciding on our alternatives?" is a question that assumes that they want to begin sometime. The question, "Have you donated yet?" clearly implies you expect them to donate.

This leads us to commentary adjectives and adverbs. *Happily, fortunately luckily*, *obviously*, and *unfortunately*, are all words that have a linguistic pattern that presupposes everything that follows. For example, "*Obviously*, this one is a higher quality machine than that one over there." What's missing in that statement is what makes it obvious. "*Fortunately*, we'll be able to serve your needs throughout the year." "*Unfortunately*, we're unable to supply you credit on the first order." What's missing is why. Because these are commentary words, they do not lend themselves to questions as in the other examples. They are only used as commentary.

While presupposition questions can be constructed and used as straight declarative sentences, putting them in question form generally will both add to their power and soften them quite a bit. This makes them easier for the client to accept without question. By stacking as many presuppositions as you can into the same sentence, you will add to the power and impact of what you are saying.

For example, answer this: How many of the beneficial ideas you've learned here do you plan on sharing with your colleagues this week?

Now that you've answered it, let's see how many presuppositions were stacked in that question.

Presupposition #1: There were multiple ideas

Presupposition #2: They were beneficial

Presupposition #3: You've learned them

Presupposition #4: You have colleagues

Presupposition #5: You share with them

Presupposition #6: You will possibly do it this week

Presupposition #7: Your brain will give you an answer automatically

Or consider: Have you asked yourself recently how many services your current suppliers should be providing but are not? If you have thought about this for any time at all it probably made you more than slightly discontent.

See how presuppositions work? Now we'd like you to write some of your own presuppositions that match the examples we've offered. This is important for several reasons. First, it will help you further understand what these presuppositions are about, and what makes them work. Second, your own participation in writing out phrases that you can use in your own business environment will help you apply these principles into productive, effective, persuasion strategies. Third, by having them written down you'll be able to practice them again and again, until they roll off your tongue as comfortably, sincerely and as naturally as can be.

The reasons presuppositions work is that they are mental and linguistic shortcuts. By weaving suggestions, commands and questions into the flow of your sales presentation you are able to embed them in such a way that they will facilitate the decision-making process, which will help the buyer take the shortcuts necessary to reach the conclusion he is striving for.

As you can most probably see, there is a clear possibility of manipulation using these strategies. Manipulation problems are much greater in the short-term than they are in the long-term for a clear reason. Short-term manipulations undermine long-term relationships. And most selling success is based on long-term repeat business and quality referrals. That is why excellent salespeople understand that it is best to be *other-oriented*. They focus on facilitating win-win choices rather than being more *self-oriented* and forcing win-lose choices. Yet even good choices that satisfy real needs will sometimes be difficult because people resist change. Also, we need to understand when presenting untried ideas we will be dealing with a certain number of fears. Some seminar leaders are fond of pointing out that the only way to grow is *straight fearward*. There is some truth in that.

If our outcomes match the outcomes of our clients and we facilitate their good choices through helping them get through some of the dysfunctional decision-making baggage they may be carrying with them, then we are indeed providing a good service. Years later the clients will still appreciate that we exerted the energy and effort to help them make that valuable choice.

If you are personally convinced of this you'll even find yourself using a very good and powerful future pace statement such as, "Several years from now you'll thank me for helping you select this." And if you're truly congruent, sincere, and well-intended your customer will nearly always agree. If, on the other hand, you're playing the sales game in an us-versus-them, let-me-take-advantage-while-I-can approach, you can still use these strategies to get agreement. But like looking at just the top of the ocean, what you will be missing are the more important things below:

1. Repeat business over time;

2. High quality referrals for even more business;
3. Customers you can turn to for advice and assistance;
4. Better cooperation should problems arise;
5. A reputation of quality within your industry;
6. Personal pride in doing the best job possible;

Without question in business we encounter some people who would lie when the truth would serve them better. But these people are working through their own distorted perspectives of fear and mistrust. Because of this fear and mistrust, they get the fulfillment formula backwards. Where they need to love people and use things, they seek satisfaction in using people and loving things. Manipulating to achieve the good things in life prevents them from achieving the best things in life. The pity is they could have both.

METAPHORS, ANALOGIES AND STORIES

"If sales presentations were suits, some would instantly fit the prospect with comfort and elegance. And some would fit as if they were off the rack in someone else's size. Even if both styles had the same material, which one would you be inclined to buy?

A major difference between most salespeople and those who are far superior is the influence strategies they use. Most have a relatively small, inflexible range of such strategies, and thus go through their sales day in hit-or-miss fashion. Yet others seem to sense how to quickly, if not immediately, size up prospects and tailor their presentations to the prospects' individual buying styles..." is the metaphor that begins this book.

Metaphors, analogies and stories are additional power tools to use when making presentations. They have a way of vividly hooking into the client's imagination and value system.

Psychologists have known for years how valuable metaphors and analogies are in psychotherapy as a tool for discussing problems indirectly in a non-threatening manner. In this way they serve to: (1) simplify things and make them more understandable, (2) present them in an interesting and memorable light, and (3) help people approach sensitive situations in a non-threatening manner. The same is true in selling.

Humorists understand the power of metaphors and analogies and use them repeatedly to delight us by underscoring unexpected similarities we have not noticed before. For example, in an episode of the TV program "Cheers," a character sums up his feelings of helplessness in the business world by saying, "It's a dog-eat-dog world out there and I'm wearing Milkbone underwear." Similarly, when asked the question, "How's business?" a friend of ours occasionally pulls out one of his favorite old analogies. "Well, business is kind of like sex," he replies. "When it's good it's really good, and when it's bad, it's still pretty good."

Here are some business examples we've heard recently:

To a slightly disgruntled client thinking about changing ad agencies:

"Taking on a new ad agency is like buying a used car. An agency can shine like crazy for the test drive and presentation. But you never really know whether you've made a good choice until you've driven it hard for awhile."

To a hospital committee deciding whether or not to invest in market research:

"You are physicians and hospital professionals. You already know the absolute necessity of professional diagnosis before prescriptions are written. What we're offering is a means of diagnosing your hospital's strengths and weaknesses. From that basis we'll be able to prescribe your best marketing alternatives."

To potential contributors to a college scholarship fund:

"By contributing to these scholarships you're planting seeds... seeds that will sprout into educated professionals... seeds that will sprout the future."

PROJECTIONS

We've already acknowledged that involvement is a key to good selling. You will recall that question techniques are certainly a good way of establishing involvement. Projections are another form of involvement. Projections are when you project the client, customer, or prospect into a situation in such a way that he or she mentally begins to experience that situation.

You can sometimes use projection techniques with the secretary outside an office to gain insight into how best to sell the boss. For example, you may be making small talk with the secretary and ask, "By the way, if you were in my situation, how would you approach your boss with this idea?" In such situations the secretary will often give you a preview of how the boss likes to buy. Probably nobody understands the boss better than that secretary, who is working with him or her every day.

Projecting the client into the decision-making process can be as simple as asking, "What do you think we should do at this point?" Or it can be as complex as having the customer physically try out a product.

In car sales, test drives are certainly a common form of projecting the client into how good it will feel to own the new car. Helping the client with verbal projections such as: "Think how good it will feel driving this car to your appointments." "Can you see yourself using this copier to save time and become more efficient?" Or, "Can you imagine the look on your child's face when you surprise her with this gift?" All of these are projections that psychologically move the prospect forward in time and intensity to experience in advance the satisfactions we're selling.

Projections serve to involve the prospect or client logically, emotionally, and/or behaviorally. Certainly a test drive pointing out fuel economy, prestige, easy driving, and safety would be hitting all three levels at one time. Whereas the question, "If you were in my shoes, how would you approach the boss with this idea?" mainly involves the logic of the situation.

By combining projections and metaphors, analogies and stories you often can capture your prospects' or clients' imagination in such a way as to help them pre-live and enjoy, appreciate, and bask in the benefits that you are offering in your sales package.

How effective is this? Have you ever identified with a character in a movie so strongly that it affected your behavior? Many people claim that after seeing Alfred Hitchcock's original "Psycho" movie, taking showers was never the same for them. They projected so completely into the shower stabbing scene that they never felt as comfortable about taking showers again. Hitchcock's genius for projecting his audience into his plots was also shown by the number of people who watched the classic movie "The Birds," and to this day eye a large gathering of birds with a certain level of suspicion.

When you use projection with metaphors, analogies and stories their power is increased. In other words, metaphors, analogies and stories are interesting. Metaphors, analogies, and stories about us (that we truly identify with) are bound to be even more so.

ENVISIONING

Envisioning is sharing of one's grand dream. This level of selling is not for all situations and certainly not for everyone. At the grander levels we find envisioning creating momentum by a leader who is very charismatic sharing his or her dream. Politically, Martin Luther King, Jr.'s "I have a dream" speech is an excellent example of how one charismatic leader's envisioning can, in time, mobilize a nation.

President John Kennedy also used envisioning to catch the imagination of America and change the course of history. The power of his words when saying, "Ask not what your country can do for you, but what you can do for your country," still rings in the hearts and minds of many who heard them.

Envisioning is seeing and sharing the fire of one's own hopes and desires in such a way that fire catches hold in other people; they see the vision and in turn pass it on to others.

Envisioning is not relegated to political and religious leaders throughout the world and throughout history. We often see it in business and sports.

Mary Kaye Ashe of Mary Kay cosmetics is an example. She had a vision of creating a "dream company" using the Golden Rule as a means to motivate and lead. Today her personality and values permeate this company, which is one of the world's largest direct selling organizations, with an estimated 150,000 independent beauty consultants following what she so strongly believed in her heart.

It's this type of belief that starts from the inside that makes envisioning so powerful. Great leaders and communicators understand it, use it, and appreciate it intuitively. In his autobiography, Lee Iococca recalls the legendary coach Vince Lombardi conveying this insight:

"Everytime a football player goes out to ply his trade, he's got to play from the ground up—from the soles of his feet right up to his head. Each inch of him has to play. Some guys play with their heads, and sure, you need to be smart to be number one in anything you try. But most important, you've got to play with your heart. If you're lucky enough to find a guy with a lot of head and a lot of heart, he's never going to come off the field second."

You can readily see the parallel between professional athletics and professional sales. We believe this capacity for envisioning is what helped make both Lombardi and Iacocca such incredible successes against such incredible odds.

Less familiar examples abound with every entrepreneur who has ever had a dream that was so real and so burning that others caught that burning desire and excelled to make the dream come true. Envisioning is a high energy and high charisma endeavor. It is single minded and it is purposeful in its intent.

PATTERN TALK

Pattern talk is a presentation skill. It's even rarer in application than envisioning. Pattern talk is using the same cadence or same pattern repeatedly in a way that is somewhat hypnotic to the listener. Pattern talk works best in presentations that are not to be interrupted.

The most common example of pattern talk seen and heard today is in the area of evangelical ministry. This is most evident in television evangelists who use pattern talk as a communication tool for influencing their viewers and moving them to action. Usually this action relates to donating money. Their programs are effective. For example, until their problems surfaced, Jim and Tammy Bakker reportedly brought in over $140 million a year. If you've ever listened to such ministers, you've probably noticed a very distinct pattern in the way they talk. Sometimes it's sing-songey, sometimes it has a calming, repetitive flow. Sometimes it has a distinctive 'UH' sound at the end of each sentence or phrase.

The sum total of this distinctive patterning and repetition over and over and over again is to actually create a trance-like state among those listening. This trance-like state is produced by repeated vocal cues. Additionally, in some cultures a pattern of physically swaying back and forth also produces a similar hypnotic effect.

Poetry also has this power because of the pattern repetition. When music is added to repetition and patterns, and the emotions, the tone, the tempo, the language, the values, the beliefs all match congruently, we find ourselves calling the influencers rock stars, and we pay them millions of dollars for how well they influence us.

Is there a pattern talk example in business? Yes. The most elegant example of this is heard at auctions. The auctioneer establishes a rhythm and cadence that is mainly filler syllables and words. Most of the words in the pattern are indiscernible to the casual listener, but the rhythm and beat of the pattern are unmistakeable. As the auctioneer gets the audience wrapped up in the pattern, he suddenly embeds commands—"Now gimme forty!"—to which someone typically responds by offering that bid. When the auctioneer has forty he continues the pattern and commands, "Gimme forty-five," moving the bid up.

If you've ever been in an auction and found yourself competitively bidding more than you intended to pay for an item that you were initially not sure you wanted, you can understand the power of pattern talk when it's combined with embedded commands and suggestions.

Another example of one who uses pattern talk is Zig Ziglar. Probably no sales training motivator in America has been more successful over the years than he. Most probably through his Southern roots and strong Baptist background, he has a very distinctive pattern talk style. Over the years this pattern talk communication style, combined with his highly developed sales skills and strongly envisioned belief system, has made him the most influential secular sales motivator in the country.

However, pattern talk strategies are not for everybody. As mentioned earlier, pattern talk is such a specialized form of presentation influence skill that it is typically used only in those environments where the presentation has a performance aspect to it.

GENERATING AGREEMENT

Another presentation skill is generating agreement. We wear three ties for generating agreement: tie-ups, tie-downs, and tie-backs. As we discuss these, keep in mind that these are lubricants to keep the flow of communication going in the direction you want. They are not fuel for your presentation. If you try to use them as fuel your presentation will sputter because *your buyer will start feeling manipulated*. On the other hand, if you use the agreement generators sparingly, only applying them when touching on key parts of your presentation, you'll find they will help your presentation run much more smoothly, often with seemingly little or no effort.

Tie-ups are leading questions that attempt to tie up some level of agreement before the real statement is even made. For example, you might ask: "Did you know that?" or "Are you already aware that...?" or, "Perhaps you have already observed that..." "Have you ever noticed the fact that...?" "Would it be fair to say that...?" "Would you agree with me that...?" "Would you agree with most experts that...?"

You'll notice that in each of these examples there is a very strong presupposition that what follows is already established as fact. By using this linguistic technique, the statements that follow each of those phrases will be lubricated to the extent that they generally will develop almost no friction. If you fasten a tie-up to something that the prospect has already told you, then you can often generate agreement on even somewhat awkward issues. Let's say, for example, that you are selling appliances, and your customer has let you know that he has looked around at several other appliance stores in your area. You might generate agreement by saying, "Since you've already looked at several other stores' inventories, would it be fair to say that you're nearing the point where you are ready to make a decision?" If the prospect agrees, then you may follow up with the same wording in order to carry you to the next level of agreement. "Then would it be fair to say that if I show you a model you like in a price range that appeals to you, we might come to agreement today?" If the prospect agrees at that point then you've set the stage for doing business right now.

If the customer suddenly rejects your agreement attempt, immediately back off. Then get back to the agreement frame by making a statement such as, "Decisions such as this take a fair amount of comparison, don't they?" That example uses what we call a tie-down. A tie-down makes a statement and then ties down agreement by adding a question at the end such as, "People are basically good, *aren't they*? We all like good value, *don't we*? We wouldn't want this to get away, *would we*? It's a beautiful day, *isn't it*?" Tie-downs are most appropriate when they reinforce something the prospect or client has already told you or at least implied that he or she believes. For example, if a couple is talking about safety locks for the back of the car, they might say, "Safety locks are something we'd be interested in because we have kids." To which you might reply, "Our children's safety is so important, isn't it?" By mirroring back what they just said and also tying it down, you've acknowledged their opinion, belief or attitude and you've supported it through agreeing with them in that manner of speaking. Both tie-ups and tie-downs are principally used just for generating agreement.

The third type of tie, tie-backs, is used for both generating agreement and clarifying. They are called tie-backs because they tie back to something your client just said or asked. Generally speaking, if you are tying back to a statement the prospect has just made you will make a statement that acknowledges and agrees and then follow it with a question that clarifies or amplifies. For example, if your client states, "Wow! I like this one," your tie-back would be, "Yes, it shows. Which part of it do you like the most?" Here you've established agreement with his or her liking it and then gone for clarification about which part in particular is impressive.

If the client asks you a question, you will generally ask a question in return and then follow with an answer. For example, if the client asks, "Do you have this in blue?" your tie-back would be, "Is blue to your liking?" Or if you don't have it in blue you might ask, "Is blue important to you?" If the person asks, "Can we have delivery by the first?" your tie-back would be, "Is delivery by the first important to you?" or, "Is the first when you actually need it?" The reason for using this question- to-a-question tie-back form is that very often customers and prospects will throw out misdirection questions in an effort to buy time or to procrastinate a decision. By using tie-backs you'll make your task easier, because a number of customers will respond with such answers as, "No, we really don't need it by the first. I was just wondering. It'd be nice to have it then, but it's truly not needed until the twentieth." Or, "Well, I like blue but it's not really that important to me."

If their issue question is important to them, and you can provide it, tell them so. If it's important and you cannot provide what they want, hedge and probe for the underlying reasons for the need in the hopes of *giving them what they want, in a different way*. For example, if their question related to service award gifts for a company's Founder's Day, you may discover award certificates could act as gift surrogates within the Founder's Day award ceremony itself. Of course, you must never promise what you knowingly cannot deliver.

As your presentation develops, tie-backs can sometimes be used as trial closes. Let's assume you've touched on most all of the important issues in a plan except the cost of it. Let's further assume that your prospect has shown a high level of interest at every stage, but you noticed some amount of questioning regarding price. You've noticed this through such statements as, "Yeah, but that could be costly," or, "Well, yeah, but you only get what you pay for." Finally, your customer directly asks you, "Is this plan going to fit within our budget?" Your trial close tie-back would be, "If it fits within your budget would you be interested in owning it?" If you get a "No, I'm just curious at this point," you would smile and use a tie-down to regenerate agreement. "That's right, there are a lot of important elements we have to satisfy, aren't there?" If you do get agreement at that point you may wish to tie it back even further and say, "So if it fits in your budget might we get agreement on it today?" A yes answer from each of you would constitute your close.

Often the questions that generate tie-backs are open questions such as, "How soon can we have it?" In those, your tie-back question needs to be framed just like their questions. "How soon would you like to have it?" you'd ask.

"On the fifteenth," they may reply.

"Is the fifteenth important to you?" is the tie-back.

To the statement, "I'd like something sporty," you might repeat back, "Something sporty?"

"Yes," they reply.

"How sporty would you like it to be?" would be your clarifying tie-back.

Before moving forward we'd like to again advise that the three ties be used sparingly. Overusing them will make your customer feel manipulated. They generate agreement best when they are used to facilitate and enhance communication, not forcefully control it.

QUIET RECAPITULATION

Now that we've developed a number of skills needed to make good presentations, let's discuss more specifically how we will offer our plan. Actually you already know. Offering your plan is simply and quickly going through all the steps you've followed so far, only you present them in recap form. For example, using all your rapport skills, you start identifying the needs that were cited, watching your client all the time for changes in composure as you mention specific needs. If the client winces at one or changes the communication rhythm you need to slow down, clarifying the cause of the reaction.

To maximize your effectiveness you will furthermore want to identify the needs in approximate order of importance, sparingly using tie-downs to bridge from one to the other and tie-up to keep the presentation in the direction you want it to go. In harnessing the objectives you pre-play how you are going to present the new material. Then you check rapport and offer a plan of how your product or service will achieve the client's outcomes.

Your recapitulation here should match the word QUIET. Did you *Question*? Do you *Understand*? Are you *Involving*? Are you *Expanding* on what they have said through questions and comments? And are you *Tying* each point together so that there is a flow and a logic in what you are presenting that matches the way your client likes to think, communicate and buy? This tying together means that at each step you have started from where your client is in terms of focus of attention, emotion, posture, tone and tempo, language, values, and so on. Next, you've used sensory-specific language to move your client from one sense to the other, encompassing as many of the see, hear, touch, taste, smell factors as are appropriate.

And third, you've tied one benefit to the next in a chain that touches every need the client shared with you in approximately their order of importance. It's important that you recognize that offering your plan is more than simply presenting, because when you get to this point you truly are *offering them the plan of what you want them to do*.

As you offer what you want them to do, you'll want your offer to be *attractive*, (which means it's in the customer's mode of buying) as well as *congruent* with mutually matched outcomes and mutually matched words, tone, tempo and so on. You will also want to include the criteria you're using to show that it's good.

Fourth, make certain your offer is easy to become involved in. This requires thinking ahead and anticipating and removing obstacles that might prevent the buyer from continuing with you until the sale is closed.

And last, make your offer simple to understand. You should be able to present it in clear, simple, bottom-line benefits and bottom-line costs. Or, as many have observed over the years, if you can't express your idea on the back of a book of matches, then you don't yet have a clear idea.

Attractive, congruent, easy, simple are touchstones that are easy to remember because they spell ACES.

At this point, it might appear to you that your presentation is actually a recapitulation and a restatement of all the things your prospect or customer has told you up to that point.

If that's how it appears to you, you are exactly on track. For it is that, and more. It's not only telling them what they told you, but it's telling them what they told you in the style, manner, and rhythm that they told you. It's using their believability sorting strategies, their criteria and their personal and business needs in such a way that you create an irresistible package for them.

Continuing with the overall sales package, once you GRIN, ECHO, and CROP the next step is to GO-RA-RA. That is GO—Gather Objections, RA—Respond Appropriately and RA—again Request Action. Yet keep in mind that while you are in your presentation sequence, you're still in a dance with your prospect, customer or client. And to maintain your customer or client's rhythm or direction you need to be constantly vigilant for interest and buying signals. Notice changes in his or her voice tones, such as "Oh, that's interesting." Asking more questions and interrupting you for clarification points is a good interest or buying signal. Suddenly leaning forward, nodding and agreeing more vigorously is often a buying signal. And even asking such questions about delivery dates, color selection, and packaging would be indications of increased momentum. Other key presentation points to recap so you will keep them in mind are:

1. Be sure your presentation follows the prospect's agenda, not yours. The key is to follow *his or her agenda to your outcome* (which, of course, should match with their outcome).

2. Be certain your presentation uses their key words as well as yours. People like people who are like them. Likes like likes. By using their words you'll seem more like them.

3. Make certain your presentation hooks their words about needs to your words about benefits. Since people buy for their own reasons, we need to understand what those reasons are as specifically as possible. Once we have that understanding, we can more easily match what we have to offer with the problems that they need to have solved.

4. Make sure your presentation addresses their needs in the order of importance to them. This means that if you have solutions to problems that they don't have, your solutions will not pack much punch. Don't waste your energy scratching where they don't itch.

5. Be certain your presentation addresses concerns that they should have but don't yet realize if, and only if, you have ironclad proof that you can solve these problems. Bringing up such points are even more important if you are the only one who can solve these problems.

6. Be sure your presentation requests and receives verification at each important point. You can get these through tie-downs, tie-ups, or tie-ons.

7. Make certain your presentation allows your buyer to talk as much as he or she wishes. People love to talk because it makes them feel important and in control. As a sales professional, you love to listen because it provides you with buyer information and personal power.

8. Make certain your presentation uses emotion adroitly, remembering that people buy emotionally and justify logically. There are exceptions to this in terms of corporate sales (for example, industrial buying), but even in these cases emotions such as liking, peace of mind, confidence, and feelings of security are still very important in decision-making processes. Therefore,

9. Always strive to make the buyer feel more secure, confident and trustful of the legitimacy of his or her needs as well as your plan.

10. Be sure your presentation involves as many of your buyers' senses as possible. The more senses involved the better chance you have of making the sale.

11. Remember to reinforce your buyer through offering acknowledgement, agreement, appreciation, acceptance and approval.

12. Remember to sell one thing at a time, one selling point at a time, one benefit at a time, one item at a time. Don't complicate your presentation by asking your buyer to handle too many variables at once.

13. Talk to people, not categories. Labels don't buy. Human beings buy. By looking past the labels you'll find yourself talking to a person who happens to be a CEO, rather than a CEO who happens to be a person.

QUESTIONS AND ANSWERS

Question: *When a customer leads with an I-don't-have-any-money-to-spend-with-you comment, what should I do?*

Answer: First, get agreement that you have something worthy of his attention when there is enough money to benefit from what you're offering. There is a chance that the person is responding emotionally to a real or perceived short-term cash flow problem. If what you are selling has long-term cost benefits, the very concerns that initially weigh heavily against your sale can tip the scale the other way when presented in light of the longer term.

Question: *When you say to avoid negative points, does that mean to avoid everything that's not positive?*

Answer: No. It means don't bring up new negative points the client has probably not seriously considered. When the customer does have strong negative concerns it's best to recognize them and deal with them.

Question: *Is it important to check rapport if I've only been away an hour or so?*

Answer: It's important to check rapport before offering your plan even if you don't part company. If you do part company even for a short interruption, checking rapport becomes even more critical. In many cases one phone call or piece of bad news can change a customer's disposition significantly enough to stack the deck against you. Checking and re-establishing your rapport-based momentum will help put the deck back in your favor.

Question: *How long should the checking rapport state last?*

Answer: In some cases, you can check rapport in just a couple seconds. This is especially true when this stage is part of an ongoing presentation. If you have been apart from the client—even for a short time—you check rapport during your brief recap of what you had covered together earlier. For example, let's say that through direct or indirect means you know that a potential client is concerned about your newness in the market and your ability to handle peak delivery times." A good rapport-building approach would be to state, "If I were in your shoes I would be asking questions about our newness in the market and our ability to handle peak delivery times. Then present your most convincing evidence of how these issues will not be problems.

Question: *Is it possible to overuse any of the presentation techniques covered here?*

Answer: Yes. Not every tool is for everybody or every situation, and even the best power tools break down when overused. We would, therefore, caution about overusing the three ties, especially with people who have a mismatch sort. Additionally, pattern talk's applications are relatively few in most people's selling environments; so are envisioning applications. But they (along with all of the techniques) are important to know for the times that they are exactly what's needed to maximize your effectiveness.

Abraham Maslow once observed that when your only tool is a hammer you treat the whole world as if it were a nail. Our observation is that the reason most salespeople don't sell most qualified prospects is the salespeople use their own favorite selling strategies rather than the prospect's favorite buying strategies. Any repeated use of the wrong approach is overuse. That's why in our seminars we teach a wide variety of techniques and strategies and the flexibility to change what's not working.

CHAPTER FIVE

Gather Objections, Respond Appropriately, Request Action and Follow Up Every Lead

GATHER OBJECTIONS/RESPOND APPROPRIATELY

Objections come with a sales presentation like a mortgage comes with a house sale. In most situations they are necessary to get the job done. Plan on getting them and plan on handling them well. It's important to stay open and constructive when objections arise. Don't argue. Do receive objections as a request for more information.

GO APE

When you get an objection listen to the customer to the end. Jumping in prematurely with a response prevents the customer from having the satisfaction of communicating effectively and the opportunity for occasionally even answering his own concern.

Effectively responding to objections is a pace and lead proposition. The GO APE part is the pacing part. Those letters stand for:

	Acknowledge		
Get Objection...	Agree or	Project	Expand
	Apologize		

In the GO APE formula, after you get objections, either acknowledge, agree or apologize (depending on the context of the objection). You'll notice that all three alternatives are acceptance based and do not attempt to push back.

Your experience in sales has possibly already told you that often customers present only part of what's bothering them when they raise an issue. This can lead to only partially answering the customers' concerns, or missing the point of their objection entirely. Therefore, it's important to get the entire objection expressed before responding so you understand what the objection really is in its entirety. You therefore will want to project the client into the situation and ask him to expand on it.

For example, if your customer's objection relates to price he might simply say, "It's too expensive." Many traditionalists would immediately start responding to that objection without even knowing how "too expensive" it is. Is it 200% too expensive, 20% too expensive, or 2% too expensive? Even worse, some will immediately try to *overcome* the objection by immediately attempting to prove how wrong the customer's objection really is. This too often ends up with either a contest of wills, or the salesperson losing so much rapport that the chances of a mutually profitable relationship are greatly impaired.

A better approach to the it's-too-expensive objection is to first pace by using this APE strategy: "It *is* expensive. How 'too expensive' do you feel it is?" Similarly, "It costs too much." "Yes, it does cost a lot. How much too much do you feel it is?"

To further strengthen your comfort with the pattern, here are some examples of objections and how the APE pattern might be used effectively:

Objection: I think the product's box looks tacky.

APE answer: So you don't care for it? What specifically do you not like about it?

(Note here the importance of specificity in correcting or working around what a customer doesn't like about something you're offering.)

Objection: Wow! That balloon payment will be huge.

APE Answer: Yes, it will be huge. Do you see this as a problem?

(Note here that what appears to be an objection, may not be one at all. Rather than going off on unnecessary tangents, you can use the APE pattern to test if you have a true objection. The response pattern would probably be similar to what follows.)

Objection: Well, it does bother me having such a large balloon payment.

APE answer: I understand. What is it specifically about having a large balloon payment that bothers you?

(Note here that even now you may wish to repeat the APE pattern once more to make sure you're understanding the full nature of the objection.)

Objection: I'm unclear about my ability to refinance it when the balloon payment comes due.

APE answer: I see. So if you were clear on your ability to refinance, you'd feel good about the deal?

(Note here how the series of APE pacing patterns has set up a trial close. It's open-ended nature, though, can also flush out some other objections which need answering as demonstrated below.)

Objection: I'm also concerned about the amount of debt I'll be carrying on capital equipment in general.

APE answer: Uh huh, would you mind elaborating on this a little:

(Note here the APE cycle begins again on another objection.)

Objection: Last time we ordered from you the delivery was late.

APE answer: I'm sorry. How late was it?

(Note here the specific question has not yet projected the customer into the probe, so it needs another step after the answer.)

Objection: It was delivered two weeks after it was supposed to arrive.

APE answer: Oh, no. I hope that wasn't too much of an inconvenience for you.

(Note here how indirectly the question of inconvenience severity is posed.)

The reason so many salespeople are knocked out by objections is they have not yet learned to roll with the punches. APE patterns allow you to avoid square blows to the chin but to be maximally effective, these patterns need to be practiced. In other words, in such performing arts as athletics, improvisational acting and selling, it takes a lot of practice to be effectively spontaneous. This is especially true in dealing with objections.

For that reason you may wish to list and apply the APE pattern to some of the most common objections you encounter. When you're pleased with the responses you will probably find it useful to practice until the responses become more like reflexes.

THE LEADING PART

Since the pacing part of objection handling does not put the customer in a defensive position, you'll often find that the objection is dropped or diminished significantly by the client. In such cases, your APE pattern will have helped the customer handle his own objection to his own satisfaction, and you can move on with the presentation.

Other times the objection has too much substance to dissolve so easily. In such cases proper pacing is all the more important because it facilitates your smooth transition into your leading sequence. The leading sequence for turning around objections follows the mnemonic pattern RPM, which stands for:

Reframe   Project   Make up a metaphor, story, or question

You've noticed how two identical pictures can look quite different because of completely different frames around them, haven't you? That's how reframing works. You take something your prospect says and put it in a slightly different context. The classic pessimist/optimist reframe is the proverbial question of whether a glass is half empty or half full. Notice the situation of the glass remains constant while its contextual frame is changed. Other reframe examples might include:

Whether a home looks *messy* or *lived in.*
Whether a pair of shoes is starting to *wear out* or *break in.*
Whether a person is *firm* or *obstinate.*
Whether a pet's greeting is *extremely friendly* or *obnoxious.*
Or whether a politician has a *social conscience* or a *bleed-
ing heart.*

To project, as before, is to put the objector into the situation you are posing. That's the second step of the RPM pattern. For example, a classic projection question is, "How would you handle this if you were in my position?" Another is, "Being a fair person, what do you think would be an equitable settlement?" Or even, "How would you feel if you were treated that way?"

The third step is to make up a metaphor, story or question which relates to the objection that has been posed. Even if you are extremely good on your feet, you'll want to consider some useful metaphors, stories or questions to use in advance of handling some of your more commonly-received objections.

Here are some examples of how the RPM pattern works. On these examples we'll use the entire GO APE RPM sequence to show how it all flows together.

Situation: A specialty advertising person has just presented prices to a shoe chain for imprinted balloons to be given to kids. The balloon presented is a U.S. made, quality balloon which costs more than most balloons in the market.

Customer: Your price is too high.

Sales rep: The price is high for most balloons. How much too high do you feel it is?

Customer: I can buy that same size balloon for a third less. (Note that we've gotten through the APE pattern at this point.)

Sales rep: I'm sure you can. As someone in the shoe business I'm sure you are all too aware that quality is seldom cheap. (Note initial reframe about quality not being cheap, rather than inexpensive, and attempt to project the customer into the analogy with the shoe example.)

Customer: Yeah, but price is price, and balloons are balloons. (Note initial reframe is disputed. It's time to drop back and pace some more with another APE pattern.)

Sales rep: It certainly appears so on the surface, yet isn't it your experience that products can look basically the same yet differ greatly in quality?

Customer: Yeah, but balloons are just a goodwill gesture, so quality is less important.

Sales rep: You're right that the quality of what you sell your customers is of great importance. Yet even for free, how much goodwill is generated by a balloon that pops in a little kid's face?

Customer: Yeah, but how often is that going to happen?

Sales rep: Not too often, I hope. But we're talking about an order of 100,000 balloons here. And if it happened to just one child in fifty, we're talking about 2,000 customers too many. Spending a little more on quality is an insurance policy on your peace of mind, your customer goodwill and your overall image of quality. But the decision is totally yours for I can find you cheaper balloons if you wish. Would you like for me to show you how there's a major quality difference in balloons so you can make your choice more easily? (Note how this might well lead to a demonstration of how the balloons withstand pressure, a demonstration of even latex distribution or other proof such as testimonials regarding the quality that goes into the product. It also allows the chance for the sales rep to come back with a cheaper product if that's what the customer ultimately demands.)

As another example here's how the GO APE RPM pattern would incorporate a question if your customer's objection centers around not having liked the last salesperson who called on him: "Mr. Former Customer, I can see you were really turned off by my predecessor. If you had a salesperson who was somewhat irritating to the point of being ineffective to your customers, what would you do with him?" (Note that's the APE part.)

The most obvious (and most common) response would be along the lines of getting rid of him. To that you would comment, "That was just the first half of what we did to set things back right. The second relates to my personal pledge to make up for past problems by doubling my efforts to serve you well. If you did that much wouldn't you feel you deserve a fair chance?"

(Note how this reframe is one that implies, we're fair and logical people just like you, plus I want to go the extra mile for you to make it all right again. The projection is part of the question about his own trying hard and deserving a fair chance. If the rhythm of the conversation deemed it appropriate, a strengthening alternative would be to add a story about some other rocky starts which would up as great relationships.

You can readily realize how powerful actual documented case studies can be to your selling efforts when it comes to making stories fit into your RPM pattern.

REQUEST ACTION

Requesting action is essential to optimizing your sales effectiveness. Absolutely essential. It's possibly even more important than rapport, which is extremely important.

For years there has been a story knocking around sales circles about a major encyclopedia company that decided to try to improve its sales force by studying the persuasion techniques of its top salespeople and teaching those techniques to the rest of its sales force. The company's executives were especially keen on studying their number one salesperson who far outperformed everyone else.

To their surprise and chagrin his technique had nothing to do with the quality and intellect which went into their volumes. His strategy was simple. Each day he would start at the top of one of his city's tall office buildings and systematically go to each office on each floor. As he entered an office he would immediately unfold his one sales aid—an accordion-folded replica of how the spines of an entire encyclopedia set would look on a shelf. Then he would look the prospect right in the eye, smile, and ask, "Ain't they pretty?" When the surprised employee would nod agreement he'd ask, "Wanna buy 'em?"

When he was told no (which he nearly always was) he would smile again, thank them and move to the next person with the same approach, then the next person, the next person, and so on. In that way he got more rejections and more sales than anyone else in the company. In a sense he was like Babe Ruth who was simultaneously the home run king and the strike out king. Of course, he's remembered for the success, not the misses... just as you are. And just like you, he knew you can't hit homers without lots of swings and lots of misses.

Ask and ye shall receive. Sounds simple, doesn't it? That's because it is simple. But it isn't always easy, because it raises the specter of being told no.

Even so, the fact remains, the best simple answer to the question of how to get whatever you want is: ASK!.

I was recently finishing up a seminar in Newark, New Jersey, when I received a message that one of my clients needed me in San Francisco that night, if at all possible. The client had already checked my calendar with my office and on the chance that I could make it, had reserved one of the last seats on the last available direct flight out.

It fit perfectly with the end of my seminar and social obligations and I arrived at the airport an hour ahead of flight time to pick up my ticket. It must have been an especially chaotic time for Continental because the line for their service counter was queued up like a long, winding snake. To make matters worse, in spite of this backup they had no provision for moving people up to make sure they didn't miss their impending flights.

The tension and irritation increased among the waiting passengers as the time continually advanced faster than the line.

At first I wasn't too concerned because of my incredibly good luck at catching flights. And with so much time and no bags to check I saw no reason to become tense. However, as time advanced I saw my prospects of getting ticketed on time begin to diminish. To my additional discomfort, my plane to San Francisco was showing an on time departure!

With very few minutes to flight time I realized that there was no way the line would clear enough for me to make it. There were still seven individuals, groups or families ahead. What's more the mood of our queued-up mob had already twice turned especially nasty when other panicked passengers had tried unsuccessfully to make their flights by jumping line.

How do you get whatever you want? That's right, ask. Time for patience and hoping had passed. It was time to start asking my way to the front of the line. With all of my rapport strategies and gentle assertiveness I began, "Excuse me. When does your flight leave? ..." and concluded by asking, "Would you mind helping me move ahead so I can make it to California tonight?" That worked for five sales in a row. Then with only one man and a couple to go, the man's answer to my opening question was, "My plane leaves in two minutes."

"Oh no!" I sincerely empathized, "You're twice as bad off as I am. You must really be feeling the pressure with me asking to get ahead to make my plane." He looked at me in silence a moment and said, "Listen, I'm probably going to miss my plane anyway. At least you stand a chance. Go on ahead."

I gratefully thanked him very much and moved ahead. Having heard his sacrifice, the remaining couple simply gestured me in front of them with a good luck wish.

A moment later a ticket agent was free, and as I dashed the length of the counter to her position a remarkable situation occurred. The seven individuals or groups (about 14 people) who had responded to my asking for assistance spontaneously burst into cheers encouraging me to hurry and make that flight.

It's amazing how often people are delighted to help you get ahead if you just ask them. Of course, for larger requests it helps greatly if you have already invested some effort in building the relationship.

In sales, as in life, rapport is certainly a great first step. Working through the system we've developed throughout this book is a good general roadmap to follow. For example, identifying clients' needs is a logical next step to building a relationship with them. For here you have the opportunity of helping them first and thus adding the momentum of reciprocity to your relationship.

Further refinement of what they want and how they want it is established through your establishing their criteria and harnessing their objectives in such a way that when you summarize those objectives, the person you are influencing lights up at how you have just expressed their needs.

Checking to make sure you still have rapport, you are ready to offer them your plan (which ideally will help them get what they want while allowing you to get what you want). Of course, there will be questions to answer as well as clarifications and adjustments to make, but as these points are resolved it is of paramount importance for you to directly request their action.

It can be as simple as smiling and asking them to authorize the paperwork, or as complex as starting at the beginning of what's been covered and reviewing what transpired point by point.

Trust your experience and trust your intuition, but we have found that if you have properly identified their needs, established their criteria for success, and harnessed their objectives, your closing procedure need be nothing more than showing how what you are proposing satisfies their needs and objectives according to their success criteria.

This was done for my wife and me recently at a Volvo distributorship we visited while spending a few days at our condominium at Longboat Key, Florida. The salesman had carefully questioned and learned what we deemed important. We had even told him about a specific Volvo at another dealership much closer to our home which we were considering.

As we looked at the car which pleased us the most he suggested we consider it in the light of what we considered important. Then he started listing some of what he had learned from us.

"As I recall, you feel very strongly about safety. You definitely want a station wagon for car pooling and traveling, you want a car that will last to the point of even being passed on to your kids when they start learning to drive. That narrows us down to one of the Volvo station wagons. You also want the best possible gas mileage. That steers us away from our turbos. You plan on using it on family trips, so you're going to want both cruise control and very comfortable seats. You know the nice thing about leather seats is not just how nice they feel and smell, but how well they wear over the years. Let's see, you wanted a light color that was not necessarily white because of this Florida sun... oh yes, and one of you feels strongly about having automatic windows. Now it seems there was something else..." he said as he glanced at the car we were considering most strongly.

"A roof rack, a good sound system and the ability to attach a bike rack," added my wife.

"That's right, with am/fm stereo and a cassette player," he smiled. "And if we can get you all that a reasonable price, you'll be happy." We smiled in agreement. Then nodding to our car of choice he said, "Let's go inside and see if we can make this one perfect for you." Which he did.

Like most people, I love being sold well and resent being sold badly. That's why buying a car from that Volvo salesman was such a pleasure. His close was simply a matching of what he had with what we wanted, presented as simply as A, B, C.

FOLLOW UP EVERY LEAD

Following up every lead starts with the most important lead you've got for receiving future business – your current client.

Many salespeople miss this point, somehow believing that once an order is sold the selling job is done. With such an assumption the first cracks appear in the foundation for a long-term profitable relationship.

SYMBOLS OF RAPPORT

Earlier we mentioned the value of symbols. Oftentimes a short note thanking a customer for his time and reassuring him of your pledge to supply excellent products and service will strengthen the feeling of mutual commitment.

A phone call a short while after delivery is also a good gesture for building the feeling of rapport and mutual commitment. Imagine an automobile salesperson calling you a few days after you bought a new car to ask if everything is all right and if you're enjoying your new car. Wouldn't this increase your good feelings toward the salesperson and the dealership?

Of course, some would argue this point questioning, "But what if some little problem was bothering them, that they probably wouldn't have complained about had we not asked?" Indeed! That's the point. Small irritations are the big irritations which haven't grown up yet. If a customer likes the new car, but is annoyed by the small rattle it developed, that small rattle will begin tracking a disproportionate amount of the customer's attention when thinking about the new car. Add a few more unattended problems and words like, "lemon," "taken," and "They'd better..." start creeping into the customer's mind. How much better it is to short circuit such insecurities by proacting to make the customer satisfied than simply reacting.

Or consider it this way. You have a 24-year-old bachelor brother who calls you to say he's just met a wonderful young woman. They met through mutual friends and spent most of last weekend together, and agreed to go sailing together next weekend. He is infatuated with her and thinks she probably feels the same way about him. Would you advise him to call her sometime this week? So would we.

BUYER REMORSE

Generally speaking, the bigger the commitment you have from a customer, the greater the chance of buyer remorse. Questions of having made the right choice creep in, and again the client is more likely to selectively perceive what is wrong with the deal disproportionately with what is right with it.

Again, symbolic gestures showing an attitude of service and commitment go a long way in making the customer comfortable with the choice. When the gesture if followed through with good value and quality service the long-term foundation is established.

Here's how a number of successful auto dealers and at least one national car finance organization proact with a particular tangible symbol to minimize buyer remorse and boost the chances of future business. Their symbolic item is a high quality brass "registered key fob." This registered key fob has a postage guarantee and an individual serial number on one side and the dealership's name and address on the other. If done properly, upon completion of the paperwork, the salesperson or sales manager will present the couple with two registered key fobs and say:

"Mr. and Mrs. Smith, we would like for each of you to have one of our registered key fobs to protect your keys. You'll notice that each one has a different serial number and a postage guarantee which we will pay. We've already entered your name and register number in our records. That way should you ever lose your keys in a way that a stranger finds them, all he'll need to do is drop them in any post box and they will be returned to us. We'll then compare your register number and deliver them to you immediately.

"That provides you with the peace of mind of knowing you have the maximum amount of chance of getting your keys back without any of the concerns of having your name and address on them should the lost keys fall into the wrong hands.

"It also is a symbol of our long-term commitment to you to provide you as much personal service and peace of mind as we possibly can. And even though you may move across town or across the country, we hope you'll keep us notified of where you are because that commitment on our part stands no matter where you move."

USER ERROR

Sometimes the problems which follow a sale are neither your fault nor your product's fault. Sometimes the problems stem from user error, and thus are your client's fault. But they are still *your* problems.

Since product users are much quicker to blame the product and supplier than themselves, it's important to acknowledge that not being to blame for problems does not necessarily mean you win the long-term business game. Therefore, proper customer follow-up also requires being certain user problems are prevented or resolved as efficiently as possible.

One rapport-oriented service manager for electrical equipment recently shared with us a strategy for handling user problems over the phone. When he gets a call that one of his systems simply won't turn on, start up, or boot up he has a series of easy procedures he covers with them on the phone. His first procedure is based on the fact that often the problem is the equipment is unplugged. Rather than risk further irritating or embarrassing the caller he'll say, "Sometimes these problems come from the plug connection being a little off. Would you try unplugging it and plugging it back?"

He says that a surprising number of callers will respond that the unplugging-replugging procedure did the trick, rather than admitting that only the second half of the procedure was necessary. He adds he learned early in his career that the worst thing to do was make a service call only to find the equipment unplugged. Whether he charged the customer or not it still cost his company either goodwill or money.

MORE LEADS TO FOLLOW UP

There's an old sales maxim which states that most sales people walk past more business than they write. When calling on large corporations, many accomplish this feat without even leaving the organization.

Again we feel it's important to underscore that the most important leads are those where you have the greatest momentum. Therefore, before looking beyond the organization itself, we suggest investigating the possibilities of increasing the amount of business you are writing with the customers you already have. This may take several forms.

Larger Orders

With additional insights into how your customers operate should come additional insights into uses for your products and services. Look at Arm and Hammer Baking Soda. They've rebuilt an empire on new uses for a staid, old product.

Additional Products and Services

Again, knowing the range of your customers' needs is a giant step toward seeing what other products and services you offer that your customer could beneficially use. Usually getting on a large company's recognized vendor list is much more difficult than expanding the range of what is sold.

Upgrade Products and Services

A taste of something better is often the start of upgraded buying practices. For example, clever printers will run a letterhead order and then run a few extra on a finer stock to help their customers appreciate the look and feel their letterheads could be conveying.

Additional Departments and Divisions

Referred leads from other areas within a large organization are well worth pursuing. The stronger the corporate unity the better it is. Regardless, in most cases knowing somebody in a comparable position in another department is far better than not. However, it's not as good as having a good relationship with someone who is well thought of or powerful (or both) at a higher organization level. Asking for personal face-to-face introductions is the key.

OUTSIDE REFERRED LEADS

The momentum of a good business relationship can even carry you well into other companies. Asking is again the most important step in getting these leads. Face-to-face introductions, introductory phone calls, and letters are all valuable tools in these cases. Least powerful, but still effective, is your word that your customer specifically recommended you call on the new prospect.

If your client is willing to write an introductory letter for you the format should be approximately the same as a good testimonial letter. It should state:

1. Why the client buys or has bought from you.
2. How long he or she has been doing business with you.
3. How your product or service has been of benefit.
4. Why your product or service is the choice over others.
5. That he or she highly recommends you.

A BIG LEAD TO FOLLOW

Throughout this book we've discussed a number of concepts—some new and some familiar. Now here's one that is absolutely crucial to your selling success: It's not what you know, it's what you do that counts. In other words, it's time for you to take the appropriate action to weave the best of what you've experienced here into your own selling environment.

As you do that you'll also find it helpful to occasionally review what you've read here. In doing so, you'll begin to notice how neatly it all fits in with other high quality sales instruction you've had, and you'll begin to notice a greater enjoyment of your customers and your relationship with them. You should also begin enjoying a higher income through your new skill applications.

AN APPLICATION BRIDGE

To speed your adaptation of the Beyond Selling concepts to your selling we've designed a field manual. Its purpose is to help you crystalize your Beyond Selling skills where it counts—in your selling environment. The field manual will help you systematically clarify your outcomes and the steps to achieve them. It will help you recognize and remember your prospects' and customers' buying patterns much more easily. It will provide a record of these patterns for later use. It will help you quickly review and apply the key concepts in this book. It will help you naturally ask better, more revealing questions. It will help you organize and tailor your presentation more effectively. And it will help you personally and constructively critique your interactions with clients.

We recommend it as one good way to bring action to your understanding. Information on how to acquire field manuals for you or your organization follows at the end of this book. Another good way to bring action to your understanding is to start consciously and systematically strengthening your rapport skills, adding additional elements as you improve.

A FINAL CAVEAT

There is a caveat about applying what you've learned here. It's simply this. If you start applying the concepts and skills presented here, starting with the functional fantasies and working all through the sales model, it won't be business as usual. You'll start noticing changes in yourself such as increased confidence in dealing with others and increased gusto for challenges. Others will notice too. And as such, not all of them will be able to relate to your new-found levels of success. As your level of achievement increases some may grumble, "Who does he think he is?" or "What's she trying to prove?" Initially this can be a little troubling. You'll also notice you have less and less time for griping, gossip and manipulative games.

Perhaps the following story will make my point more clearly. A friend sent it to me some years ago and it has become my favorite parable. It's about a turtle.

"I remember from when I was a very much younger turtle that I had a friend who was not quite like the rest of us. He was always wandering off by himself when he grew tired of the games that we never ceased to enjoy.

"One day he found a very large balloon and some bicycle parts, and he built himself a flying machine.

"We were all very excited about his flying machine and perhaps a little fearful, for no turtle had ever left the ground before.

"Laughing at our fears he climbed into his flying machine and soared off into the sky, waving at us from a great height. Each day he boarded his flying machine and spun off into the sky. And each day his words grew more difficult to comprehend.

"Fearing he was a little mad we decided to ignore him and continue our games. One day he disappeared into a bank of clouds and was never seen again.

"From time to time I hear rumors from passing strangers about my friend. Some say he crashed into a lake and went straight to the bottom. Others contend he grew ambitious and flew directly into the sun.

"But me? Somehow I think he's still up there in his flying machine seeing sights that no turtle has ever seen before."

That's the punishment and that's the payoff. Yet what you've got here isn't a flying machine. It's merely the blueprints for a flying machine—a flying machine of your own construction and your own personal options. Yet if you will take appropriate action and apply what we've shared here, it's our sincere hope and belief that sometime over this next year you'll look at all you're accomplishing, smile to yourself and say, "Yes, lately I've been seeing the sights that the other turtles have only dreamed of."

We wish you Godspeed in soaring that high. Good luck and good selling.

QUESTIONS AND ANSWERS

Question: *How much license should we take in actually making up stories for our RPM strategies?*

Answer: About as much as a minister does in the average sermon.

Question: *I always have trouble thinking quickly on my feet, so I'm uncomfortable with coming up with good APE and RPM responses on the spot. What should I do?*

Answer: It is hard to be quick and indecisive at the same time. That is why we recommend that you plan and practice APE and RPM responses in advance. There's even a section for doing that in our *Beyond Selling Field Manual*. Once you have a feel for the general pattern you'll be amazed how easily your responses flow.

Question: *Do many salespeople share my reluctance to ask for the order?*

Answer: Yes indeed. Fear of rejection is very common and it's the cause of many salespeople stopping short of requesting action. Yet some insurance industry estimates are that sales can be increased by around 30% by directly asking for the order at the end of the presentation.

Question: *Do you have any psychological strategies for getting over such fears as asking for the order and call reluctance?*

Answer: Yes we do, but the strategies could fill another book (and perhaps will) and many are experiential (rather than simply instructive) so they are less suited for print than for more personal contact such as either audio tapes or our seminars where direct contact, coaching and personal tailoring are provided.

Question: *How long should it take to start naturally incorporating the elements in this book in such a way as to start noticing great improvement?*

Answer: In some areas, such as rapport skills, you are likely to start experiencing noticeable improvement within days after you begin regularly incorporating the pacing patterns into your life. The key is incorporating what you've learned into your workaday world, for that's where it counts.

Other patterns may take a little more time and even more than one reading. And all of them take practice. After all, what we're sharing here is not a flying machine, but the blueprints for a flying machine of your own construction. It's your actions which will determine how high you soar.

Where do we go from here?

If you are interested in Beyond selling Seminars or author appearances for your company please call or write:

Success Sciences
5205 E. Fowler Ave.
Suite 125
Tampa, Florida 33617
1 (800) 767-5700

THE NEW BEYOND SELLING PLANNER AND DEVELOPMENT GUIDE LIFE TIME PLANNER FOR SUCCESS

The Beyond Selling Planner and Development Guide is a powerful tool for organizing and planning your success.

If you adopt the FUNCTIONAL FANTASIES from Beyond Selling and develop a level of mastery with Beyond Selling skills and techniques you will have a life time of success.

CONTENTS:
CALENDAR: Month at a Glance
DAILY ACTIVITIES: Calls
       Activities
       Beyond Selling Developmental Activity
GOALS: Goal Achievement Worksheet Part I
    Goal Achievement Worksheet Part II
NOTES:
FINANCES: Record Keeping
NAMES, ADDRESS AND PHONE NUMBERS
BEYOND SELLING:
• Functional Fantasies
• Types of Pacing
• Predicates
• Linguistic Tips
• Pre call Checklist
• Key Questions
• Cost/Time/Quality Checklist
• Outcomes: Questions to discover what your prospects want.
• Questions to elicit Sorting Styles
• Sorting Styles Grids
• Objection Handling
• Presentation Self Checklist
• Follow Up/Follow Through Checklist
• Symbols
• Client Letters

AUDIO CASSETTE: How to get a fast start on maximizing your
        personal influence.

CALL TODAY! SOUTHERN INSTITUTE PRESS INC.
1-800 633-4891

Order Form

Yes! Please send me _____ *Beyond Selling Field Manuals* at $29.95 each plus postage and handling.

Book total .... $ _____ . ____

U.S. Postage and Handling @ $2.50 each $ _____ . ____

Canada Postage & Handling @ $5.00 each $ _____ . ____

Europe Postage & Handling @ $10.00 each $ _____ . ____

Order total .... $ _____ . ____

VISA # _____ Exp. _____

MasterCard # _____ Exp. _____

Signature _____

    Order from SOUTHERN INSTITUTE PRESS, INC. by check, VISA or MasterCard:

    SOUTHERN INSTITUTE PRESS, INC.
    Box 529
    Indian Rocks Beach, FL 34635
    (813) 596-4891